LETTERS

Letters for Auntie Flo

Journal of a reluctant disciple

Graham Young

Marshalls

Marshalls Paperbacks
Marshall Morgan & Scott
3 Beggarwood Lane, Basingstoke, Hants., UK

First published by Marshall Morgan & Scott 1983

ISBN: 0 551 01086 X

Printed in Great Britain by
Richard Clay (The Chaucer Press) Ltd,
Bungay, Suffolk

LETTER TITLES

ACKNOWLEDGMENTS

This book was born out of experience. When asked to write something on radical discipleship I was tempted to stick to theory. Instead I have written about experience – much of it my own. True it has been refined by much reading, talking and biblical study, but I hope that people will first be able to relate to the experience and then be caused to think and grow, developing their own discipleship. It is the 'Journal of a Reluctant Disciple' because the life God calls us to is far from easy. I hope you will not hold back.

My thanks to Alison and Frank White for their support and encouragement, to Valerie Lindsley for all the typing and most of all to Alison Moore who helped, advised and encouraged. Thanks also to John Gladwin for his foreword.

Time spent on this book has been yet more time away from my family, Jill, Emma, Ben and Sam, my thanks for their help and support too.

Graham Young
Durham – May 1983

FOREWORD

Becoming a Christian not only changes our relationship with God, it also changes our relationship with the world in which God has placed us. Accepting this and coming to terms with its meaning for our values and our action in the world can be both painful and troubling. The call of God to grow into the image of life reflected to us by the risen and glorified Son of God has to be faced out in all aspects of our human existence. How are we to do this?

There are three essential parts of the learning process in obedient Christian discipleship. First, we need to use the resources given us in the Gospel as witnessed in the Bible. We need to hear the Word of God. Second, we need the help and stimulation of other Christians. We must test our hearing of the Word of God in the fellowship of the Church of God. Third, we need to experience the world in which God has placed us. We hear the Word of God and test it out in the Church in the context of a life which is open to all that is happening in the world. All three parts go together in the development of a Christian life. To be exposed to this process of learning is to open the door of our lives to the possibility of radical changes in our attitudes, values, and activities.

In these letters of David to his Auntie Flo, Graham Young takes all these parts seriously in challenging us with the call to a radical form of discipleship. In one sense this book is easy reading. It is full of humour and humanity. It is written in a manner and a form which make it available to a wide audience of Christians concerned to obey the call of God in the world today. In another sense this is a hard book to read. The searching analysis of contemporary issues and the nature of the call of God in them will provoke reactions. The reader is likely to be angry and even confused as cherished attitudes and priorities are put under the searchlight of a radical Christian judgement. These letters call us to change, and they undermine any way in which we try to protect our lives from the implications of our commitment to Christ. It is a discomforting book. Yet disturbance can be the work of the Holy Spirit of God – and who knows what He might do with us if we are ready to follow where He leads?

All who are concerned with social responsibility in the Church will welcome this book and its vital challenge to us in our discipleship.

John Gladwin
Secretary to the Board for Social Responsibility
of the General Synod of the Church of England.

1: Settling in

Dear Auntie Flo,

Well I've made it – if that's not too exalted a statement, sitting here in my digs bedroom with nothing better to do than count the remains of swotted flies on the wallpaper! (I wonder if they ought to have a decent burial?) Perhaps I ought to settle for a more conservative comment such as, 'I'm here', or even stick to talking about the weather, which seems to be my landlady's principal topic of conversation. Over dinner this evening I had to endure a luridly detailed description of what effect various states of the weather had on equally various parts of her anatomy from her bunioned foot to the hole in her eardrum! All of this is accompanied with statements such as 'Of course it's a known fact that . . .' I haven't actually seen any copies of *The Lancet* or other such medical journals about the place but the certainty with which she makes these statements would seem to indicate that they are supported by at least such an authority. Well, enough of Miss Greensit, though no doubt with such interesting conversation she will find her way into my letters at some later date.

After the tremendous send-off you all gave me the other Sunday morning after the communion service, I made my way straight to the station to catch the one o'clock train. I think it was only when I had got on the train and settled down that it all came home to me. I was actually leaving you and all the other people at South Street church to go and make my fortune in the big city! I suddenly realised how much that church and all of you meant to me. Having lived on my own since Mum and Dad died it's not that aspect of moving away that bothers me, it's moving away from the fellowship in the church and all my friends there. Well I'm here (I think I've said

ST JONES'S

this before somewhere), and I've got to get on with it.

Don't worry, though, Auntie Flo, I'm all right really. It's just that I have occasional moments of panic when I realise that there isn't anybody round the corner where I can pop in and have a chat. I suppose the other factor is the time I have on my hands. At home I used to be out or at least busy every evening and all weekend. If it wasn't the youth club it was the prayer meeting or the mission-planning committee or putting yet another window back into the church hall. (I suppose now I've gone they'll finally invest in bullet-proof glass or something – mind you, the Bash Street Gang will find a way!) Here, apart from going to look at the occasional flat to rent, there is absolutely nothing to do – hence the preoccupation with burial services for flies. Still, things could be worse – I could be sinking into sin and debauchery down at the local which seems to be the principal occupation of the other resident here. He has been here longer than me and seems to have mastered the art of minimum involvement when Miss Greensit gets going on her bunion. (What is a bunion, anway?)

I am, however, spending some time investigating local churches. I never realised how difficult it was to get in on things if you don't know what is happening. Last week I tried to make some inquiries about churches but didn't get very far, mainly because they all seemed to be locked up. I suppose ours (I mean 'yours'!) is too, but you don't realise how off-putting that seems until you come as a complete outsider and don't know what's going on. I tried asking Miss Greensit, in order to change the subject before she got going on her medical problems again! I thought also that it would be a good witness to her and perhaps be the beginnings of a more fruitful discussion. Perhaps I should have known better.

In reply to my question about good churches in the area, she started talking about her father. This puzzled me at first, until I realised that she was referring to the local Catholic priest! She said it was a very good church and that I ought to go along. She even offered to wake me early on Sunday so that I could get to eight o'clock mass! I explained that I wasn't a Catholic, but she said she was sure the Father wouldn't mind – especially if I mentioned that she had sent me! She then proceeded to extol the virtues of the Pope's local representative. He's fairly new and 'much better than the old one' – principally, I gather, because he's secured a licence for the church hall so they can now have drinks with their bingo session! She also mentioned something about afternoon meetings for pensioners and an unemployed group. She didn't have a lot to say about his preaching of the gospel. Isn't it funny, the idea some people have of what a good church is?

Well it looked as though I was going to have to suck it and see, so I planned a round of churches to visit for the next few Sundays. Last Sunday I visited two of the more local ones. Oh boy! I felt like coming home to you right away. The one I went to in the morning was remarkable only in that people still went to it at all. It was so dead it was unbelievable. My hand was shaken by a wet fish when I went in and I was given a hymn book which, as a first edition, was probably quite valuable. However, the fact that it had no back and half the pages were missing probably somewhat reduced its worth! The organist seemed to suffer from sleeping sickness and to specialise in playing little-known tunes to well-known hymns. During the seated bits half the congregation looked as though they were asleep while the other half, if the heavy breathing was anything to go by, actually were. The preacher read a sermon which, judging by the illustration, he had written some years previously. I can't remember what it was about. As the youngest person present by decades rather than years, I left quickly before they asked me to open a Sunday school or something!

In the evening I went to a totally different church. They were quite a lively bunch with a number of younger people and couples – some were even playing guitars. I thought things were looking up. However, just before the service started a clip-board was passed along the pews. When it got to me I found it was a petition reminding me of my Christian responsibility to keep our area a nuclear-free zone. The lady next to me gave a rather disapproving glance as I declined to sign it and stashed it in the umbrella stand at the end of the pew.

The service was much more lively than my morning experience but the prayers were all about riots, Northern Ireland, and the Third World. Even the sermon was very political. It seemed more like a Labour Party meeting than a church service. Not that I have ever been to a Labour Party meeting, I must admit, but I have been to some good church services and that was not one of them! So the search goes on, as they say. I have got some more churches lined up for next week – they're a bit further away but they do look more promising.

I haven't said anything about the job yet but there isn't time now. More about that later. I am sorry if this letter seems to have rambled on, but I do miss being able to talk to you. The phone is in Miss Greensit's living-room and so makes telephoning rather difficult. I couldn't have told you all that interesting information about her bunion for instance! Don't worry about replying to my epistles, though a postcard every so often might help – just to let me know you're still there!

I hope all is well with you. Do give my love to everyone at South Street.

God bless

Love

David

2: Seeking the faithful

Dear Auntie Flo,

It's me again. Have you recovered from reading my last little contribution to English literature?! I promise not to say anything about Miss Greensit – or not at this stage anyway! (She's been to the chiropodist, by the way – she calls him the 'Kropdis'! But that's enough, not another word . . .)

It's all been happening since I last wrote. First of all I have found a flat! There are just the formalities to sort out still. It's been quite a job, I can tell you, and you wouldn't believe some of the places I've been offered or the rent they ask for them. Knowing how much I could afford to pay, I visited some flats in that range. They were either so small that you couldn't swing a mouse in them let alone a cat, or they were in really terrible areas.

One was really nice inside with two bedrooms and a really big living-room, but as soon as you stepped outside the front door it was awful. The whole road was tatty with graffiti all over the place. Some of the houses were 'daubed' with the most amazingly gaudy colours. The noise was as deafening as the colours were blinding. From inside the flat it sounded at one stage as though someone was being half strangled to death outside the front door! But when I looked out everybody seemed to be laughing so unless they had a particularly sick humour I presumed that all was well. As I beat a hasty retreat down the road I saw a house with stereo loudspeakers actually pointing *out* of the windows and turned up full blast! It was mid-morning but there seemed to be lots of people, men included, just hanging about on the street corners – nearly all of them were black. I'm certainly not prejudiced, as you well know, Auntie Flo (I'm still keeping up with my sponsored child, by the way), but I decided that it was not the place for me to live.

FLAT to LET
S/c
CH
double bed.
fully equipped.

I've done some pretty hard praying since then. I knew that God wanted me to move down here but where did he want me to live? I can remember when we talked about whether I should move or not, you said that if I was faithful to God then he would be faithful to me. Well I can really say that he has been and things have, amazingly, fallen into place.

It all started when I found a local Christian bookshop. I was just wandering around the town when something (or someone!) made me investigate a narrow back street and there was this little bookshop. It had a big 'Smile, God loves you' sticker on the door and I can tell you I did – even though it was shut! I called back the next day and had a long chat with the woman who ran it. She told me all about the local churches and invited me to her own. Isn't it tremendous that if you know Jesus then you've automatically got lots of friends?

Anyway, not only did she tell me about churches but she also mentioned a flat to let in a house owned and lived in by a Christian couple from her church! So armed with the name of Mrs Jennings from the bookshop, I shot off round there that evening as soon as I could. I told them all about myself and the move and we seemed to hit it off right away. They are a lovely couple called Sandy and Diane. Sandy is a town planner and Diane is a sixth-form teacher. The house is in a smart part of town called Deynes Park and the main part is done out really nicely with stripped-pine furniture, those hanging basket things with plants in, wall-lights and small print wallpaper. The bit they are renting out is a sort of granny flat at the side but it is completely self-contained. It is about fifteen minutes' drive from town – I suppose twenty minutes or so on the bus – but I think it will be worth it.

They said I could have the flat and I was certainly very grateful, even though it will cost a bit more than I wanted to pay. It has only got one bedroom but otherwise it is just right. So I am moving in next week when we have settled the formalities. I will let you know the full address and telephone number later.

Then came Sunday and I could at last go to their church. Miss Greensit didn't seem too worried that I had missed mass though she did cool noticeably when I told her I was going to Claygate as everyone calls it. anyway, I got off to a good start for the 10.30 service, in fact it was an even better start than I thought because the service wasn't until 10.45. Still, it's good to be early and get yourself in the mood! It also enabled me to meet a few people before the start. Sandy and Diane introduced me to their friends and I had another chat with Mrs Jennings. Everybody was so friendly that it felt like home right from the start. We had some good lively hymns and a tremendous prayer and praise time – it was just like South Street. I almost expected to hear Mr Thomas strike up (slightly off key of course) with 'Turn your eyes upon Jesus'.

The preacher preached from 2 Corinthians 5.17: 'When anyone is joined to Christ, he is a new being'; and he stressed the need for us to be 'new beings'. It's something that I have held close to me as I have begun to establish myself here, the need for people to see that I *am* a new being. I don't simply do what other people do or say, but what Christ wants me to. It was something to take with me as I started work on Monday. Anyway, as you can no doubt tell, I was pretty taken with the church and the people there. I went back on Sunday evening and found out about mid-week meetings and so on. There seems to be lots to get involved with – I went to the prayer meeting on Tuesday, and to the area house group on Wednesday with Sandy and Diane.

The group meet at the house of a couple called John and Amy Wilson. It's a tall, old terraced house with very large rooms and is a bit nearer the centre of town. John is the leader of the group and it was excellent. One of the group led us in a Bible study and then we had a time of discussion and prayer. It was a good opportunity to get to know people better and to tell them a bit about me.

Well, enough about church. The thing I really moved down here for was, of course, the job and it started on

Monday. I think it is going to work out well. There is much more potential here than in my last job. As you know, it is an insurance brokers and they deal with all kinds of insurance. I am going to be working in the office to begin with, getting to know the ropes and how the firm operates. Later on as I get established and make contacts I am going to be moving over to the personal insurance section, life insurance, assurance and so on. That's what I really want to get into – then I will get out to follow up leads and make my own contacts.

I'm in the office at the moment (on my lunch break, honest!) and it's not going too badly at all. The people are very nice and we get on fine – so far anyway. Mind you, I think that is going to be the problem. How am I going to show these people that I am joined to Christ and therefore a new being? I suppose the drinking, lying, flirting and swearing are all there, although not very obviously so. Therefore it's easy to steer clear of them without seeming different. But that is it, it is not obvious that I *am* different. We are very alike really, eager, hard-working, punctual, ambitious, etc. I think it is going to have to be something that I do rather than *not* do. I have decided to try and make opportunities with each of the people in the office, to talk about Jesus and what he has done for me. Then people will know that I am different.

Well, Auntie Flo, God *has* been faithful and things are going well. I am really looking forward to getting involved at church and getting into the system at work. It is pretty exciting and a great challenge to be a 'new being' in a new beginning.

Talking of challenges I don't think I can go any further without mentioning Miss Greensit again. I thought I had got somewhere with her because she muttered something about going to church. However she wanted me to go along with her one morning to the Catholic mass. I managed to get out of that one and asked her to come with me to our church but she wouldn't, it's a real shame.

Well, I will probably be leaving Miss Greensit next week. Even though I haven't been here long I think I will miss her in a strange sort of way, in spite of the regular updates on her bunion, etc. I will also have to cook for myself. Still, I suppose that will cut out the arguments about how thick the custard should be. Living with people with different views does make life rather difficult, and I suppose that goes for more than the custard! I think Jim (her other lodger) will be glad to get rid of me, with the hope of getting a drinking partner next time. He also seems to have extended his disappearing act to avoid not only Miss G's bunion but also any discussion about 'rligum' which he reckons one can take or leave. He seems to prefer leaving it, and as far behind as possible!

I hope all is going well at South Street. No doubt it is. Times like these make you realise how dispensable you are. Remember me to all the gang and thank them for their prayers.

Look after yourself,

God bless,

Love David

3: Two sides to a story

Dear Auntie Flo,

I must tell you the saga of our sewing-machines for Sri Lanka! But you had better hold onto your armchair because I never thought that helping someone in the Third World could be so complicated.

Last weekend we had a special meeting at church on the Third World. A lady from an overseas aid agency gave a talk and showed some slides about their work with poor people in Sri Lanka (apparently it's what used to be called Ceylon). This agency is supplying sewing-machines so that the village women can produce their own clothes and sell some to supplement the families' poor wages. We thought this was a great idea and decided to raise money to buy some of these sewing-machines. It was suggested that one of the house groups should arrange the fund-raising. John Wilson, our leader, volunteered us!

So this Wednesday our group met at John and Amy's and we decided to get down to our plan of action right away. However, to our amazement, one of the group objected quite violently. I say 'to our amazement' because she is one of those people who seem to be quite 'into' the Third World and such like. She ranted on about treating symptoms and not causes and how irrelevant it all was. At which stage I didn't know if I was coming or going. You would have thought this project was right up her street but obviously she was Not Amused, as they say. So someone asked her to explain and there began my longest house-group meeting yet! Break off for your second cup of tea at this point if you so desire, Auntie Flo, because there is a lot more to come.

Jill (that's our ranting lady of the long night!) said that the reason these ladies in Sri Lanka had to supplement

their wages was because they were not paid enough for picking our tea in the first place – in fact, that very tea which you are probably now sipping! She reckoned that as we pay for our tea then we are paying their wages. We could not deny our responsibility for the fact that these tea-pickers did not have enough to live on. Once we know about this and carry on regardless then we are actively supporting the oppression of these people.

Did you know that a female tea-picker gets paid about nine rupees (that's 50p) a day? She does get a bonus dependent upon the weight of tea she picks, but when 1 lb of rice costs two rupees, it's not much, is it? A room 8 feet square is home for a family of seven. Well, we were all rather stunned – to say the least – by this statement, and when Amy Wilson got up to break the ice and make some drinks, nobody moved a muscle when she asked who wanted tea! Poor Fran – who they say drinks about three gallons a day – was horror struck.

What stung most, I think, was when Jill said that it was hypocritical to send sewing-machines to Sri Lanka and not do anything about the links we already have with these people through our daily dose of tea. To stop drinking tea is not the answer, we need to see that our Sri Lankan tea-pickers get a fair deal. It seemed a bit strong to me and rather impractical. Someone put my thoughts into words by asked, 'Yes – but how?' Jill said we could start by buying W.D.M. tea. W.D.M., I thought – we drink more? Well distributed money?? But I was wrong on both counts. Apparently it is an organisation called the World Development Movement which campaigns for justice for the world's poor. They are involved in importing tea from a tea estate with better conditions for its workers. W.D.M. also tries to pressurise the big tea companies, many of which are apparently British-based, to pay their workers better wages. They get people with shares in these companies to go to shareholders' meetings and vote to make the companies take a more responsible attitude to their workers in the Third World.

Well at this point I said it all sounded rather political

to me and I wasn't sure whether we should get involved in such things. Jill exclaimed, 'But it's all in the book!' and reached for her enormous bag. I wondered what she would bring out (the illustrated version of Moa's little (!) red book or the full works of Karl Marx?

To my surprise she surfaced with a rather battered copy of the Good News Bible (illustrated family edition). 'Oh!' I said. 'Yes,' she said, 'It's all in here.' (What, even my P.G. Tips? I thought.) She reeled off a host of verses from the Bible that showed that at least the prophets of the Old Testament thought that religion had got something to say about trade. Apparently Ezekiel (28.16) told the King of Tyre, 'You were busy buying and selling, and this led you to violence and sin.' In Hosea (12. 7–8) it says, 'The people of Israel are as dishonest as the Canaanites; they love to cheat their customers with false scales'. The most insulting one was from Amos 4. 1–2. 'Listen to this, you women of Samaria who grow fat like the well-fed cows of Bashan, who illtreat the weak, oppress the poor, and demand that your husbands keep you supplied with liquor! As the sovereign Lord is holy, he has promised, "The days will come when they will drag you away with hooks; everyone of you will be like a fish on a hook."' It makes you think, doesn't it? Fancy calling someone a cow of Bashan.

Then somebody said, 'Ah, but that's all old Testament.' At which point she threw in a verse from James 5.4; 'You have not paid any wages to the men who work in your fields. Listen to their complaints.' As she seemed to be getting into gear on the New Testament, John thought he would silence her by saying that you can prove a lot of things by quoting isolated verses. At this point Jill closed her Bible in seeming despair. But she was far from beaten.

'Don't you see?' she said. 'When Christ came, he came to announce that God's kingdom had arrived. All that the prophets of the Old Testament were looking towards and entreating the people to live by was complete in him and his work. His work was to bring both spiritual and physical deliverance. Separating the spiritual from the physical is foreign to the Bible.

'In Luke 4. 18–19 he declared his work as bringing good news to the poor: "He has sent me to proclaim liberty to the captives and recovery of sight to the blind; to set free the opprressed . . ." Jesus began that work of God's kingdom here on earth and when he left us the Holy Spirit was sent so that we could carry on the work.'

Well, as you can imagine, that was the beginning of a rather long discussion and it was all pretty powerful stuff, not exactly the way in which yours truly is used to thinking. But it was hard to argue a convincing case against at least finding out what is going on. Jill made it sound very simple but I am sure it is a lot more complicated than it seems. For instance, someone said that they thought the Sri Lankan tea estates had been nationalised and were now owned by their government. Jill said the British firms still controlled all the selling, buying and shipping etc. and had a lot of influence in what went on, and do own tea estates in other places like Bangladesh and Kenya, but she agreed that we needed more information. The point was also made that these tea-pickers are poor and need help *now* – any moves to increase wages are bound to take time. So we agreed to organise a Saturday fair at the church to raise money for the sewing-machines. But we would also investigate what is being done about the tea-pickers' wages, lobbying of the companies, and so on. Perhaps we could then have a display at the fair about it and even use W.D.M. tea for the refreshments and offer packets of it for sale. Someone at the meeting knew someone else who was in contact with the Christian company called Traidcraft which sells the W.D.M. tea and some special coffee and crafts made by people in the Third World, so we thought we could have a stall selling these goods.

John heaved a great sigh of relief at this point hoping that at last something was sorted out and we could all get off home before the milkman arrived! I hauled myself up from my seat on the floor and left with a numb leg and a numb brain. I wasn't sure whether it had been sorted out or not. I got a lift home with Sandy and Diane and I can tell you that they were not very happy about it – much too political for them. I am undecided, but could see Jill's point. I suppose it is hypocritical to be doling out charity with one hand and yet helping to create their poverty on the other. But is it really the sort of thing that Christianity is about? Would Jesus go to shareholders' meetings to protest about poor wages? I told Jill that I wasn't sure that she had got her theology right. Which, on reflection, was probably a bad move because she has promised to talk to me about it sometime!

Well I'm sure you have had enough of this by now. I'd better go and have my supper. I hope cocoa is allowed!

Love David

4: Anti-flow

Dear Auntie Flo,

Do you remember that I told you Jill had offered to 'fill me in on her theological position'? Well, it has happened – fool that I am for showing interest! She persuaded me to go to a meeting with her to listen to some guy called Sands talking about 'radical discipleship'. John and Amy Wilson came along as well – as my house-group leader I think John felt a responsibility to guard my mind! It was quite a mind-blowing experience, I can tell you. He opened by saying he was going to talk about Auntie Flo which, as you can imagine, took me aback somewhat! Fortunately I refrained from telling Jill that I knew you personally and instead sat in rapt attention.

To begin with he talked about repentance. (What's new about that, I thought.) He said that all the prophets from John the Baptist way back into Old Testament times called for repentance. Jesus' first message to the people was about repentance; the apostles' teaching and preaching after Jesus had ascended was about repentance; and I thought of my old Bible Class teacher – you remember Mr Thompson? He was always going on about the need for repentance. (Looking back, I suppose some of us did have a fair bit to repent about! But anyway, on with the show.) It was a bit like a show as well, because he had this big white board (as opposed to a big black board if you see what I mean) on which he started to draw a diagram. I have copied it out for you here so keep your thumb on this bit and I will try to explain it all to you, and I mean try!

As I say, first of all he talked about repentance. That's bubble number one at the top of the diagram. I tried to think about how Mr Thompson had defined repentance, but it got rather limited to being sorry for something I

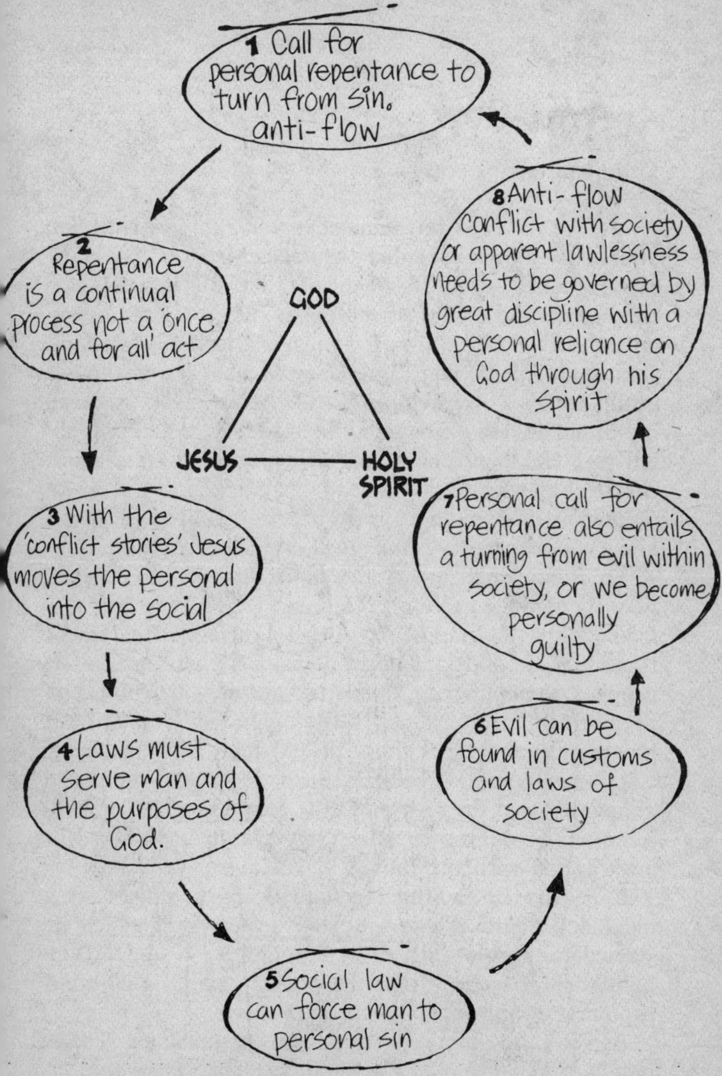

Anti-flow chart

had done and asking God's forgiveness. But this guy was saying something more than that. He said that that view was too specific. OK, so you lie or something: you do have to be sorry for that, but sin is something much deeper than the occasional action we do or don't take. Even if we can't think of anything that we have done wrong we are still 'sinners' and need to repent, because sin is an attitude of mind. It is the attitude that puts me instead of God at the centre of the world; that thinks of me first instead of others. God calls us to turn around from that approach to life and through Christ he leads us to repentance and enables us to go in the opposite direction. He enables us to put God at the centre and to think of others before ourselves. That is 'anti-flow', turning around and going in the opposite direction to that which we would naturally follow. Repentance is more than the negative act of being sorry, it is also the positive act of changing our minds, our direction. It was at this point that it hit me! Our Mr Sands was not going to be talking about Aunti Flo at all but about 'anti-flow', going against the tide and all that sort of thing. There I was, thinking you had gained well-earned fame at last when it was all a case of mistaken identity!

Mr Sands mentioned that passage in Romans 7.15 where Paul says, 'I do not understand what I do for I don't do what I would like to do, but instead I do what I hate.' (There's a tongue twister!) That's the conflict that we all experience, between wanting to do what God wants and yet so often finding ourselves dictated to by that inner force which makes us do something else. Being aware of that force within us (which is sin) and turning from it to do what God wants is what repentance is all about. That is anti-flow, fighting against the normal flow of our innermost urges and going in the opposite direction, against the tide.

I remember once trying to make my way to the front of the church at South Street after a packed service, while everyone else flooded towards the exit at the back. Anti-flow, going against the tide, suddenly seemed a very apt picture of what trying to be a Christian is like.

So that took us on to bubble number two in our diagram, about repentance being a continual process. I must admit I had never really thought of repentance in this way before. I think the changing direction aspect of repentance for me was something that had happened when I committed my life to Christ and it sort of got left there. You repented and then became a Christian, but after that? I was a bit hazy about what role it played other than being sorry for a specific act. Mr Sands, however, was very clear in saying that repentance, 'changing direction' or anti-flow, didn't just happen once but was something that we must claim from God again and again. That bit in Romans about Paul not doing what he wants to do is as true a statement about life after conversion as it is about life before conversion. Even after I have said I want to follow Christ I still don't always do what God wants me to do. Therefore I have to repent again and again.

My instinctive reaction is to put me first and not God. Therefore my first reactions are always suspect – not necessarily wrong, but always questionable. Now this doesn't mean that we have to look over our shoulder every time we do something, but it does mean that we have to think a little more about the things we do, especially those things that we sometimes just take for granted.

I tried to think of the sort of 'things' Mr Sands meant and the subject of friends came to mind. Coming down here to a new place I have been making a lot of new friends – or at least a lot of new acquaintances. I have only really got friendly with a few people who think the same way as me or like doing the same things. That is the natural way we go about making friends, I suppose. It seemed, however, that what Mr Sands was saying was that the natural or normal way of going about something doesn't mean it is right – in fact it means it is suspect! I shelved that one at the time, but I have been thinking about it since. As I say, I have made a few good friends who think like me or do things like me – they do me good and confirm my view of life. Like Sandy and Diane or

John and Amy, I suppose. But perhaps there are some people who would benefit from my friendship even though, on the face of it, they are not going to do anything for me. For example, the bloke at work who is in charge of our section is a real pain, he has got a chip on his shoulder and thinks everybody is trying to get at him. He gets people's backs up and takes everything the wrong way even when you are trying to be nice to him. So everybody has given him up as a bad job. Nobody speaks to him unless they have to. But perhaps I ought to persevere with him – even though it is not going to be easy and even though the rest of the office will think that I am just trying to get in with the boss. Perhaps that is what Mr Sands means by anti-flow – not necessarily doing what comes naturally!

The point about friends also illustrates very clearly what was said about repentance being a continual process. We don't just make friends once! We need to be always open to repentance so that, as we deal with the decisions we must constantly make in our lives, about friends or anything else, we can deal with them not by our own or other people's instincts but by God's promptings.

Well I feel as if my arm is going to drop off with all this furious scribbling. I hope you don't mind me pouring all this out to you – it really helps me to sort out my ideas. It is, however, getting rather late and I ought to get to bed. I'll need all the sleep I can get if I am going to do anything about my boss, I can tell you! I've hardly started on this anti-flow diagram; please keep it until next time and I will try and finish it off then.

Thanks again for all your prayer and support. I feel in some ways that I am beginning to settle in here now. The flat is fine and the job is going well. But this talk by Mr Sands has given me an awful lot to think about. By the time I write again, I may be a bit more sorted out.

Look after yourself and God bless you.

Love David

5: Second instalment

Dear Auntie Flo,

I nearly got carried away then and wrote 'Dear anti-flow' – which must give you some indication of what has been occupying my mind over the last week! But before I launch into that again, let me say that I have been working on my boss – loving your enemies and all that sort of thing! Well the results have been amazing: he seems to hate me more now than he ever did! My anti-flow principles are taking a severe beating I can tell you. The last thing I 'instictively' want to do is to carry on trying to befriend him. However, I *will* carry on (he says with a fixed grin on his face). After all, nobody said it was going to be easy. I suppose Christ was crucified for it.

Still, let's not get carried away. I will keep you informed and meanwhile back to our Mr Sands. I hope you kept my delicately drawn anti-flow chart from the last letter? I will try and zip through the rest of it tonight. Mind you, as I only managed two bubbles last time, the indicators are not too good!

The first two boxes state the need for personal repentance and for seeing the anti-flow process as continual in our lives. Bubble number three talks about Jesus moving this personal concept into the social realm. Now this was when it really began to get interesting: Mr Sands pointed out a side of Jesus that I had not really seen before. He pointed out a set of incidents recorded in Matthew, Mark and Luke which he called the 'conflict stories'. In Luke, for instance, there are six of them which come between chapter 5, v.12 and chapter 6, v.11. In five out of the six the actions of Jesus and his disciples lead them into conflict with the Pharisees. This was not by accident or by mistake; Jesus openly and knowingly confronted those who were the religious – and in some senses

the political – leaders of his day. The Pharisees were very watchful of Jesus and they tried to test him. Jesus, being aware of this, challenged the accepted norms of the day in front of them. He took an anti-flow approach, not just in terms of personal ethics but also in terms of the law, rituals and habits of Jewish society.

In the call of Levi in v.27 of chapter 5, Jesus demonstrates his attitude to sinners. It was not the normal attitude of Jewish society, which was to shun them and have nothing to do with them. On the contrary, he went and sat down to dinner with them. His was an anti-flow response to a social issue.

In the early part of Luke 6, Jesus tackled the law about the Sabbath. There were very strict laws in Jewish society about what could and could not be done on the Sabbath. Certainly you could not work on the Sabbath, and that included rubbing together ears of corn to get grain to eat – even if you had missed Sunday lunch (or Saturday lunch, if you see what I mean)! Well apparently this is exactly what the disciples did and they were challenged by the Pharisees. You can almost see the Pharisees rubbing their hands with glee – if *that* was allowed on the Sabbath. Jesus replied for the disciples to the Pharisees, which in itself is an interesting point because it would seem that he was claiming for his followers (and that includes us) the same right to the anti-flow approach as he had. Jesus told them (as recorded in Mark, which some say is the original text) that the Sabbath is made for man and not man for the Sabbath. So he was not denying the need to observe the Sabbath but saying that if certain man-made aspects of that observance became more of a hindrance than a help to man then that was not as God meant it to be. Jesus even quotes an episode when David broke the law by eating the bread from the temple that had been offered to God. This is what Mr Sands meant by his bubble number four on the diagram: laws must serve both man and the purposes of God. If they did not, it would seem Jesus claimed the right, in certain situations, for himself and his followers to break them.

This takes us on to bubble number five. The second incident related in Luke 6 is again another Sabbath-day story. This one is about the healing of the man with the paralysed hand in the synagogue. The Pharisees were there again, watching: would Jesus heal the man or wouldn't he? (You can just imagine it, can't you, all sitting there with bated breath waiting to see what would happen.) Some people even suggest that the Pharisees brought the paralysed man there deliberately.

Well, Jesus was aware of all this and even though he realised what the reaction would be, he called the man to the front. He asked whether the Sabbath law allowed them to help or to harm. Of course there was no answer to that and so he healed the man. It would seem that Jesus was saying that it was not just a choice between doing good and doing nothing at all, but between doing good and doing evil, helping or harming. Doing nothing is not just a passive act but actually means doing evil by condemning this man to further suffering with his paralysed hand. As bubble five in the diagram shows, the structure of that society was actually calling Jesus as an individual to do evil by preventing him from doing good.

Well this was rather mind-blowing for me as well as for the Pharisees of the day. Their reaction, in v.11, was to go away in an unholy huddle and discuss what they could 'do' to Jesus. I didn't know what to do either, but the Sri Lankan sewing-machines immediately came to my mind. I remembered Jill talking about our willingness to perpetuate a system that kept the tea-pickers we employed in abject poverty. We didn't go out of our way to point out the iniquities of the system, but were content to send out a few sewing-machines. Our relative inactivity in respect of the structures was not a passive act, according to Jesus, but actually entailed us in doing evil. The sewing-machines didn't affect the system in any way, so a refusal to 'help' in that area would mean that, in Jesus' words, we 'did harm'. Throughout all this I kept looking at John Wilson but he seemed to be taking it all rather calmly.

That takes us on to bubble number six in the anti-flow chart. Jesus recognises that the tendency within us to do evil, of which we must repent, is sometimes enshrined in the systems we create so we need to repent from these as well. That is to turn from them and seek to go another way, God's way.

To illustrate this, Mr Sands went on to talk about the story of Babel, or the tower of Babylon as the Good News Bible calls it, in Genesis 11. Now I would not have thought for one minute that the story of the tower of Babel fitted in here, but what Mr Sands had to say was very interesting. Apparently the people at this time after the flood were still a wandering people. Some of them, however, came together at a place they called Babylon and decided to build a tower or city, only the second recorded city in the Bible. They had decided to settle down. Everyone knows the story of how they couldn't understand one another, confusion set in and the whole project collapsed. People had come together as a corporate, social body, but because of the tendency to sin, the system that they tried to establish failed and the people were again scattered. There was no one individual who could be blamed for that failure. The structures were either inappropriate to this new situation or actually caused evil. Whichever it was, the structures themselves failed to honour God by preventing the people from living together in love and justice, and in that sense they embodied sin. We are called to repent, to turn around from this manifestation of sin just as much as from any personal tendency we have to dishonour God.

This understanding brings us to bubble number seven on our anti-flow chart. The accepted norms of our society can, in as much as they are developed by man, embody the sins of man, or even when they are inherently good, they can be used by man to do evil. We cannot therefore blindly accept the society's structures or its customs and habits (i.e. the way in which we use those structures). They must come under close scrutiny to see that they are honouring to God, to see that justice is done and love prevails. If they do not, then we must act, because if we do not, as in the story of the man with the paralysed hand, we commit evil by not doing good. Not to take the path of anti-flow, of repentance, is to support the *status quo* (that which already is in existence). It is either anti-flow or *status quo*, there are no in-betweens. If the *status quo* is dishonouring to God, then we dishonour God.

Well, as you can imagine, one or two people were getting a bit hot under the collar at this stage, me among them! I mean the theology seemed to be all straight from the Bible, but I had never heard things put in this way before. It seemed to be knocking at the very basis of society. But then I suppose Jesus *was* knocking at the basis of society, turning it upside down and all that sort of thing. So if our normal approach to life is being questioned what is there left that is certain? God I suppose. But it can't be right to question laws, that leads to anarchy: we need laws to enable us to live together.

Those were the questions that went through my mind, but Mr Sands had not finished. In fact he went on to cover this very issue of the need for laws and customs. He said that the tower of Babel story shows that without a realistic social framework the city collapsed. The problem comes if we assume all laws to be totally acceptable and are not aware of the need to repent from their sinful aspects. We need constant vigilance and the willingness to go against the flow of society when we are so prompted by God.

At this point, one gentleman, who seemed to be slowly changing from flushed pink to deep purple around the collar, shouted out, 'What about Romans 13?' (Mutterings of 'hear! hear!' in the background!) He meant of course the passage that says that everyone must obey the state authorities. Mr Sands said that of course he agreed with that – what he had just said about the fall of the tower of Babel indicating the need for state authorities showed that he agreed with it. But, he said, later in that passage Paul shows the very specific role that authorities have, that of praising those who do good and punishing those who do evil. Even an occupying power could do this, as Paul had recently experienced, therefore authorities must be obeyed. However, in this passage Paul does not make any comment on what we should do if the authorities cease to praise the good and punish the evil. It is Peter and the apostles in Acts 7.29 who say that when the laws of the civil order conflict with those of God then we must obey God and not man; and Jesus himself said that we must pay to Caesar what is Caesar's but to God what is God's.

I am not sure that our man with the rainbow neck was convinced but I began to see the point. I was still worried, however; how do we avoid simply lapsing into anarchy, with people deciding left, right and centre to go against the accepted norms of society and against the law?

Well first of all Mr Sands said we should not get things out of proportion. We are not talking about breaking every law of society simply because it is man-made. There is a need for laws: some kind of structured system, as opposed to any one particular government, is ordained by God. Rather, we must look on the other side of the coin – we are anti-flow people because we want to go *with* the flow of God's will. We must therefore be steeped in the love of God and his word, and have a strong personal relationship with him so that we can follow his will. We are not negative people but rather we are positively working towards the establishment of the kingdom. Only when society comes into conflict with that, must we become anti-flow.

It is through God's Spirit within us that we are prevented from wanton lawlessness. This is the essence of bubble number eight in the chart, and it is why we come in a circle back to number one, the need for personal repentance. The way of anti-flow is frought with dangers, and it could become an excuse for complete lawlessness. We lead a very exposed life when there are so few things we can take for granted. Therefore we must have that personal relationship with God and we must constantly be open to repentance. We started with this call for repentance and I remember Mr Sands reading from Mark 1.15 where Jesus says, 'The right time has come . . . the kingdom of God is near! Turn away from your sins and believe the Good News!' I suppose what all this means is that if we turn away from our sins then the kingdom of God will be near. This kingdom is something to do with our living relationship with God, through which we are able to challenge and go against those things that are wrong in ourselves and in society and do what is right. We will be loosening what ties us to ourself and the world in order to depend on God.

The radical discipleship view of the Christian life approaches our involvement in the world from the roots of the problem – that's what 'radical' means. They are man's sin, sin's embodiment within society and man's relationship to society and God. The triangle in the middle of the chart is apparently meant to show our dependence upon the Trinity. The possibility of repentance is a gift from God. Jesus showed us what sort of life we should be turning to. The Holy Spirit guides us in our present pilgrimage set in this world but with the vision of a better life that is possible.

Well it was all a bit hard to take – but perhaps that is itself part of what Mr Sands is talking about. I should not just rely on my natural reactions – How does it feel? How have I always interpreted it? etc. Perhaps I should actually put a bit more thought into it, and that's what I have been doing ever since. I went to have dinner with John and Amy Wilson the other night and we had a long chat about it then.

The sermon we heard that first Sunday morning I went to Claygate kept coming to mind: 'When anyone is joined to Christ he is a new being.' I have been worried about showing everybody that I *am* a new being when perhaps the problem is that in so many areas of my life, I am not! I do not repent of those areas, I have not 'turned round' or 'changed my mind'. If I really was new it would show and I would not have to create opportunities to tell people about Jesus because they would ask why I think and act as I do. I limit my 'being different' to a few personal and fairly petty sins such as lying, cheating, swearing, etc. (Now I'm not saying they're not important, Auntie Flo. Don't worry, I haven't started stealing the office stamps and lying to my boss!) But most of the other people in the office wouldn't do those things either. Perhaps there are other more basic areas of my life that I need to change – by not facing these I am actually limiting my effectiveness in evangelism.

John, Amy and I talked a lot about this and I found them very helpful. They said they have been thinking about this for some time and that the talk had actually confirmed some of their thoughts such as questioning the assumption – which seems to be fairly widespread – that the aim in life is to make more and more money, to get a bigger and better house and to have the best car we can afford (or the H.P. will let us have!). I'm sure that is the basis of life for many people in our office including me. That is what binds us together, the struggle to reach the sales targets, to beat the targets, and I am no different. But perhaps that is not what God has in mind for me, perhaps he is calling me to be a new being in this. It might well affect the way I work and the way I treat people, both customers and the other staff. Do I persuade people to buy policies they don't want or need – in order to reach my targets?

Perhaps there are other things too, issues that I just take for granted, like my innocent cup of tea, which need to be looked into a lot more carefully, if I'm to follow the anti-flow approach!

Well I think that had better be it for now. I have a feeling that life is not going to be so simple from now on. But I have a certain excitement in that it could lead to a much closer relationship to God as I look to him for what is acceptable or not rather than to my own instincts or the 'normal way of doing it'.

God bless you,

Love David

6: The first test

Dear Auntie Flo,

Thank you very much for your letter. I had completely forgotten that you had been out to India as a missionary all those years ago. I can understand, as you say, that in some ways what the Indian people got from the British-owned factories and tea estates was better than what they had before. The problem is that the conditions do not seem to have changed a lot since those days. It is interesting to read that looking back you feel a lot of assumptions were made that our way was right and their way of life wrong and that the Christian faith you took was too linked with the British culture. I suppose that is one of the big problems I have been coming up against and that Mr Sands was talking about. The problem is sorting out what are the basic elements of the Christian faith and what are the traditions that we have put on top. I do realise that not all traditions are wrong but I suppose it is important to keep hold of the fact that even with good traditions there may be better ways of doing things. What start off as new and visionary ways of life can easily become unbending ruts that are no longer appropriate, and we can easily lapse into the way of the world. Hence anti-flow, constantly being aware of the need for repentance, 'turning around', 'changing our minds'! Well I'd better not get back on to that. It really has been very interesting though. I have been studying those conflict stories in Luke and I've had some really good discussions with John and Amy. I have broached the whole area with Sandy and Diane at the house here once or twice, but I did not get very far with them. I think they are getting a bit worried about me!

I don't think I told you that John and Amy have got two kids called Daniel and Sarah. They are a right

MONTHLY STATEMENT
NEW
ITCH
ITCH
ITCH

handful. Sarah is five and at school now and Dan is just three and goes to playgroup, or 'playgwoup' as he calls it. I offered to take them down to the park last Saturday afternoon to the swings. I tell you I have never been so frightened in all my life! I was sure I was going to take them home with at least a cracked head apiece. All those flying swings and great high slides, still they seemed to enjoy themselves. I found it very interesting watching them play with other children. The Wilsons' house is in between the posher area of town called Deynes Park (where I live) and a downtown area called Brice. That's the area which I described to you where I went to view a flat. This park seems to serve both areas and so there were a number of black kids there. The children, however, didn't take any notice at all – they just mixed in and played quite happily together. You'll be glad to know we all got back safely, and a great afternoon was had by all – well all of *them* anyway!

My big problem this week is that I've been thinking about buying a car. Now that I have this new job and as I am getting paid rather more than I was before, I decided the time had come to get my own four wheels. I have been thinking about it for some time now, even before I came here, and have saved some money for a deposit. I've looked around at the car showrooms and have got my eye on one or two different models.

When I told one of the blokes at work what I was thinking of buying he laughed and said that I ought to get something with a bit of 'oomph'. 'Oomph', I said? 'Oomph', he repeated, 'you know, something that's going to really go, something with a bit of acceleration, speed – appeal even.' Appeal? I thought. I'm not sure who or what it was to appeal to, but I held my tongue. It turned out that our Tony is a bit of a one with the cars and ever since our conversation, he has been persuading me as to the appeal of various models. He reckoned that as I was still single and therefore had more money to spare (!), didn't have to bother about carting a wife, six kids and the mother-in-law around, and as I would obviously want to impress the ladies (that must be where the appeal comes in!), I ought to think of something a bit more sporty. What about a Lotus, an MG, or at the very least a custom Ford!

Well, I must admit there were one or two cars which in my more wilder moments I quite fancied. Other friends in the office seemed to have really nice motors. I visited a few more showrooms with the indefatigable Tony who reckoned he 'knew a good car when he saw one' and chatted about the sort of credit limit they would give me.

I got rather excited by a really nice GT model with fuel injection (I know it sounds more like a rocket than a car but Tony says it's good). I told the salesman I would think about it – much to Tony's disappointment. Anyway, we were near John and Amy's so I thanked Tony for the lift and dropped in to see them.

Inevitably the discussion got round to my car buying and Amy said that she hoped I was applying anti-flow principles to my decision. Her remark was more in fun than anything else, I think, but it was this remark that made me think – was I actually applying my Christian principles to car buying or was I more concerned about what I wanted, what Tony thought and how the rest of my colleagues saw me?

We talked about my reasons for buying an expensive German car. It was true that I could afford it – just about! But by going right to my credit limit would I be tying up money that could be used for other more important things? If I bought a cheaper car, would that enable me to give more to the church or to some other worthy cause? What about the Sri Lankan sewing-machine fund? Was it a direct trade-off between the number of sewing-machines that went to Sri Lanka and my car with 'oomph'? Would the insurance on such a car be so expensive, and I so up to the hilt in H.P. payments, that I could only insure it for myself to drive? Therefore, would I never be able to lend it? Would it be too smart and precious for me to want to lend it anyway? Would such a sporty car be any use for doing things in the church or community, carrying loads around, collecting things? I had laughed at Tony's criteria for car buying, but perhaps he was just being more honest. Perhaps deep down I too want a car that would impress – other people and myself. An expensive car would be a sign to myself and others that I am getting on and being 'successful'. I'm not going to be doing lots of long car journeys each week so I don't really need a fast, comfortable, reliable car.

In fact, do I really need a car at all? That was the question we finally came down to. I suppose it was one I should have answered right at the beginning. I certainly want a car but do I really *need* one? Both church and the office are on good bus routes and during this period that I am purely office-based, I don't need a car for my work. So, why not use the bus? Amy even suggested a bike – it wouldn't use up valuable petrol and would certainly be a lot more healthy as I sit at a desk all day. I could just see myself trundling down to the office on an old 'sit-up and beg' bike with a basket on the front and parking it next to Tony's snazzy 'oomphmobile'. I could chain it to his bumper. He would probably talk me into trading it in for a model with drop handle-bars, ten gears and a racing stripe on the water bottle!

Well, so much for my smart little German car. Amy thought it was hilarious. I said I wasn't sure if we weren't taking things a bit far. I mean, we will all be out on the streets living in shanty huts if we're not careful! She laughed again. Still, it certainly made me think.

Next day I told Tony I had decided not to buy the German car. He didn't try to change my mind – he thought it was a little over-priced anyway (he didn't tell me that the day before!) and said he would look out for something else. That evening I went with Sandy and looked at a rather old estate car. I paid for it in cash and insured it for any driver. Next day Tony was not amused, even when I said he could borrow it if he needed to shift any belongings! But it certainly provided an interesting topic of conversation in the office when I tried to explain why I'd bought it.

I'm really enjoying the freedom of being mobile, it will also mean I can stay in bed a bit longer – no bus to catch to work! Well, I will have to go now. Sandy has promised to show me how to check the points and the plugs – I'll be stripping the engine down next!

Love to you and all at South Street,

David

7: Not counting the cost

Hello Auntie Flo,

This is 'rent-estate', your friendly trucker and frustrated Lotus Elan driver speaking! They actually announced in church on Sunday that if anybody needed help moving things (or people) they should see me. It sounded as though I had bought an articulated lorry! Still, I have been called upon – even if it was only to take the Wilsons' cot to a single-parent family in Brice. I say 'only' but the lady certainly seemed to be grateful. It's amazing what you can do, with a little help from your friends.

Well, life goes on. Work is quite busy at the moment. You would think that everybody waits to insure their cars at the same time of the year: we have been rushed off our feet recently. This means of course that the tension builds up a bit and my boss gets even more ratty than usual. I am trying to be friendly with him though. I made him some coffee the other day and he could hardly believe his eyes. I think he reckoned I had put arsenic in it or something! In fact I wondered if I had when I saw the face he pulled – I had forgotten the sugar. Well you can't win them all!

Last night I went to a meeting with John Wilson. It was rather a last-minute affair – he left a garbled message with Sandy and Diane. They said it was a talk about being persecuted for the faith. Do you remember that meeting we had at South Street about Christians in Russia? Well, I found that quite interesting so I thought I would go along to this one. When I got there, the speaker turned out to be a black guy called Steve Asago, and I wondered how he had come to be in Russia. When he started talking I realised the meeting wasn't concerned with Russia at all, but South Africa!

SOUTH AFRICA

Apparently Mr Asago was born in South Africa and has lived there for the best part of his life. About six months ago he fled from the country because his life was in danger. He said that the police had threatened him because of his Christian faith. I tell you, life has never ceased to surprise me since I came down here. I always thought that South Africa was a Christian country? I know there is a lot of bad feeling about South Africa but being persecuted for your faith was a new one on me and hardly seemed credible – especially the bit about being threatened by the police. Mr Asago wears sunglasses – even indoors. I don't trust people who wear sunglasses all the time so, all in all, I was rather sceptical. What did he mean about being persecuted for his faith?

First of all Mr Asago said he needed to give us a run-down on the situation in South Africa. It seems quite involved but I'll give you those details I can remember. You probably know all this – but it'll help me to remember if I write it down! There are lots of different races of people in South Africa, categorised as whites, Asians, Coloureds and blacks. Now there are more than five times as many black people (if you include Asians and Coloureds) as white people, but the whites are very much in charge. They make up the government and black people are not allowed to vote. Now these people have all come from different origins and for different reasons to South Africa. Just as in Britain, people have come not only in the last few decades but through many centuries past, to invade or to settle or to work and so on.

In South Africa the white people have decided that they can't give black people the vote because they would then take power, which the whites feel 'they are not ready for'. In fact, they would upset the whites' very privileged position, rightly demanding a share in the wealth and government of the country. The blacks (and most of the rest of the world) are obviously not at all happy with this white view and want the vote for black people. So the whites in South Africa hit on this cunning plan called Separate Development or apartheid. By this system the black people are separated off into their various races and pushed out of the 'white areas' into lands that are called their 'homelands'. They are welcome to come back in and work for the whites of course, but only with the whites' permission.

Now remember, the whites are in charge, and what they say goes. So when it comes to the carve-up of the land in South Africa to create these homelands, guess who gets the best bits? It isn't the blacks, I can tell you. The blacks apparently only get about 13 per cent of the land even though they make up about 85 per cent of the population – and it tends to be the rotten, infertile land. Mr Asago showed us a map that outlined the homelands. All the edges of the homelands were marked by wiggly lines with some bits separated off from the rest, where all the good land had been carefully skated around. Now the South African whites can send any blacks they don't want out to these homelands and away from the white cities. You get the terrible situation that families are sent to live in these homelands where there is no work, and so the man has to travel hundreds of miles to get work. He can only do this under contract – or he will not get a pass – and the contracts last for eleven consecutive months. He only sees his family for one month a year. They, meanwhile, have to eke out a living on poor soil, usually in terrible housing (or tents) and hope that he sends money back and that he himself will come back at the end. He lives in terrible conditions in the city for poor wages, where he is open to all sorts of temptations and constantly fearful for his job.

The whole system seems to be weighted against anyone who is not white. I only managed to get a few figures down. I was particularly struck by the annual spending on education per child: whites get 640 rands per child, Asians 297, Coloureds 197 and blacks 68!

I have often heard mention of South Africa and apartheid but I don't think I had really understood what it all meant before. But, the point was how did this all tie in with Steve Asago being persecuted for his faith by the

South African police? He still had his sunglasses on and I wasn't sure.

Well, he went on to say that the whites in South Africa were having a very good time. The country is very rich – an amazing amount of our gold comes from South Africa as well as diamonds and a number of other valuable materials. With the black people so well controlled and no effective union movement, they also have a cheap source of labour. So, to say the least, the whites – if nobody else – are rich and comfortable. Therefore they are going to make sure that things stay that way, and they have a very elaborate and powerful system of police, secret police and army to help. Anybody who tries to resist them is branded a communist and dealt with very seriously. Steve Asago has experienced the 'very serious' treatment.

Because of his Christian faith, he explained, he believes that in God's eyes there is no differences between people, even though their skins may be different colours. This is not just a spiritual truth, but physical too. The whites have no right, simply because they are white, to lord it over blacks, or anybody else. The basic system is unjust and therefore unchristian. Not only that, but the system causes hardships and injustices that he believes, apparently with many other Christians in South Africa, have to be spoken out against. So that is exactly what he did, in whatever way he could. He wrote letters, talked to people, went on demonstrations and joined with some of the many Christian organisations that are trying to get the system changed.

These organisations speak out against the censorship of the media that prevents people knowing what is really going on. They complain against the pass that all blacks have to carry and against the system that keeps some men away from their families for eleven months of the year. They protest about the terrible housing conditions in which many have to live and the uprooting of whole communities to be transported to the homelands. They demonstrate against the ill-treatment of people by the police, the torture and the mysterious deaths in custody.

Steve Asago's problem was that he spoke out too much. People noticed and he became the object of police attention. He was taken for questioning. He was 'ill-treated', as he put it, and interrogated for long periods under bright lights which have permanently damaged his eyes. Suddenly my thoughts about his sunglasses burnt my mind. I suppose that is what you get for making snap judgements.

Finally he was set free but with the warning that if he came to their attention again he would not get off so lightly. He might find himself having a 'fatal slip' in the prison showers. However, his belief in God and his burden for his fellow people would not let him keep quiet, so Steve decided to leave the country and carry on his work from outside.

What impressed me most about Mr Asago was his very clear *Christian* conviction about what he was doing. He said that as he stood and watched the home of a poor black family being bulldozed and them being loaded on a lorry to be carried off into the middle of nowhere to a tent and no sanitary facilities, leaving the father behind, it was not just the tears of the mother and the screams of the children that made him lie down in front of the bulldozer: it was God.

As I listened to this small, quiet man I suddenly realised what it is to be persecuted for your faith. It is more than being laughed at in the school playground or dismissed as being wet and rather irrelevant at work, it is being hated because you challenge all the world stands for. Just as Christ was hated by the Pharisees who plotted against him. I realised that saying the sorts of things I said about buying a car could make some people very annoyed because they and their values are being challenged. Being persecuted for your faith isn't something that just happens in Russia, it would seem it happens in South Africa. Perhaps it *should* happen here too. Perhaps there are conflicts between our faith and our society but as Christians we have chosen, however subconsciously, to close our eyes to them and maintain our comfortable position and avoid persecution. We are not aware. We do not listen to Christ's call for repentance in so many areas of our lives.

You know, Auntie Flo, I don't think I ever thought so much about my faith before I came down here. My brain hurts! I don't mean to deny what happened at South Street – it was very real to me. But then it was more about *what* I believe; now it is also about *how* I live that out.

I am still rather confused, but I must admit more things are beginning to hang together now. We stayed behind after the talk and had a long discussion with Mr Asago and some other people there. Someone asked him about violence: It seemed like the sort of trick question the Pharisees threw in! Is it legitimate when opposing such a situation? That started off a tremendous discussion and I think the questioner got more than he bargained for. Still I had better not go into that now or we'll be here all night – next time perhaps.

Well, here endeth another letter from the deep south. I hope you are keeping well. How is your arthritis these days? I hope you bad leg is not playing you up too much in this weather. Do remember me to all the crowd at South Street. God bless you.

Love David

8: The horns of a dilemma

Dear Auntie Flo,

My mate Tony the ton-up kid sidled up to me at the office today and asked if there was any chance of my collecting a settee he had bought second-hand because it wouldn't go in his car! It was particularly funny because I think it's the first time he has talked to me since I refused his advice and bought my 'old banger', as he called it.

'Glad to be of help', I said. 'Thought the old banger might come in handy sometime'. I think he is talking to me again now.

I said I would tell you what happened in the discussion after the meeting with Mr Asago last week. It turned out that the chap who asked him whether violence was justified in a situation like that in South Africa was a pacifist and so had rather strong views on the subject. But, it turned out, so did Mr Asago.

'It depends what you mean by "justified"', he said. (Oh! Not one of those questions, I thought, how do I *really* know this is a pen I am writing with, etc. etc.) 'If you mean "Is violence ever right?" then I think we could say, "no, it is never right".

'However', he went on, 'injustice is also never right. In South Africa we are faced with injustice every day. Some people say that all peaceful means have been tried in order to change the system that creates the injustice and they believe that the only thing left now is violence. They believe there is a straight choice between violence and continued injustice and that even from a Christian view the right – that is, the least evil – decision may be to choose violence in order to change the system and to create justice. The Christian principle of love must be brought into play when one considers the options: even if

violence is never right, it may be the most loving course, given a choice between two evils.'

Well, as you can imagine, this got our pacifist friend rather disturbed. I must admit he was not alone – I felt rather bewildered. The pacifist chap (I never found out his name so I'll call him Mr Pacifism) pointed out that the whole Christian faith was based on the sanctity of life, that Christ's life was dedicated to love no matter what the cost, that his mission was all about turning the other cheek and loving your enemies, not killing them.

Rather disarmingly, Mr Asago agreed with that, but said 'That's right, but it was at "no matter what the cost" to *himself*. Christ was willing to suffer anything, even to die, so that others might live. But he did not mean his actions or lack of action to cause suffering to others. Christ never withdrew from situations that might free others from suffering, even though they might be painful to him. Those Christians who are called to violence do not enjoy violence: it is painful to them and they believe it is wrong. But in the fallen world they recognise it as the lesser of evils, that, after all other means have been exhausted, will free others from suffering.'

Things were really getting going now and, for a pacifist, Mr Pacifism was a pretty aggressive talker. I thought we were going to need a referee.

However, before Mr Pacifism could protest, Mr Asago carried on to give some examples. 'What about Israel?' he said. 'It was violence that brought the present State of Israel about and Mr Begin was a terrorist before that (or a freedom-fighter, depending which side you were on). What about Zimbabwe? The injustices of the rebel State of Rhodesia would still be there if people had not taken to violence as a last resort. One minute Mr Mugabe was a hated terrorist, the next he was a well-respected Prime Minister. White people get very hot under the collar about black guerrilla fighters but they treat as heroes the resistance fighters of the Second World War. People have strange double standards, often based on excessive nationalism and racism.'

A rather sly dig, I thought.

'In all these situations,' Mr Asago said, 'people have lived under injustice, tried all peaceful means, and in the end resorted to limited violence to bring about justice.'

Well that was a gift for Mr Pacifism who jumped back into the fight with, 'Ah, but how can you limit the violence? Everyone knows that violence breeds violence and still more violence – it's a vicious spiral. How do you know that the injustices you are trying to defeat are not going to be replaced by worse injustices?'

Mr Asago was ready for that one, and replied, 'We're not talking about just anyone being let loose with a machine-gun where he likes, you know. That, I don't support at all. We are talking about properly organised, in some cases representative, groups who are controlling what happens and who have a plan for government when they suceed with their struggle. Now I'm not saying that they will be perfect, of course things will go wrong, just as they do with all governments. It is only where the system that they propose is patently a more just system, that a group can be supported by Christians.'

When I could keep up, I found the whole thing fascinating. I must admit I had never really thought about it very deeply before. Looking back, I think my instinctive reactions had been just what Mr Asago described. I tut, tutted with disapproval when we heard about terrorists in Rhodesia but I had rather got caught up with the Falklands war and wanted our boys to show the Argentinians a thing or two. I suppose there looms good old anti-flow again. I had taken my view from the general opinions of people around me, what was said on the television and so on, rather than thinking about it in the context of my faith.

I could see what Mr Pacifism was saying though. Jesus did seem to be about peace and turning the other cheek and that felt right. However, I could also see very much what Mr Asago was saying. Peace is the best thing, certainly, but in a fallen world justice may have the edge over peace because of the role of love. It's all right me saying that I am going to keep my hands clean and not get involved in violence, but where that means that I condemn others to suffer that can't be right. I suppose its like Jesus breaking the law of the Sabbath to heal the man with the withered hand. Love was more important than the strict letter of an otherwise good principle.

Mr Pacifism was not to be beaten, however, and jumped in with, 'How can you say that all peaceful means have been exhausted? That's a very subjective judgement.'

He dared Mr Asago to get out of that one. Mr Asago agreed – again! 'Somebody or some group of people, ultimately, have to make that decision and yes, it is subjective. But it is not made without a great deal of agonising, especially for a Christian. He knows that he is breaking a principle that is otherwise good. But instead of criticising us for the great difficulties in which we find ourselves, why don't you help and stop us getting to the stage when we have to choose to break the law? At the present time comparatively few people in South Africa are engaged in violence to overthrow the state. Most of the violence comes from the government trying to keep the black people out of power, by oppression. However, more and more people are feeling that the time is coming when all peaceful means will have been exhausted. Those who try to change peacefully are being met with violence even to the point of death. Your concern that we should not take to violence would really mean something if you, in Britain, were willing to suffer to bring peace and justice now, before it is too late. Would you put yourselves out, even just a little, to protest about our situation and to bring change now, peacefully, before you force us Christians to strain our relationship with God by having to take the path of violence?'

That hit Mr Pacifism right between the eyes – a straight knock-out. 'Well, it's been nice talking to you but I've got to go now,' he said, and wandered off looking dazed. The whole discussion only took about twenty minutes but I think it completely changed my ideas about violence and war. I think I do believe that there could be a just war, such as the struggle of black South Africans if, God forbid, it ever got that far. But I'm no longer sure about the Falklands. OK, so we were fighting for the right of 1,800 people there to decide their own future. However, it did seem to have much more to do with reacting to the insulting of the British Bulldog. Last stand for the Empire and all that sort of thing. I don't know, though, I'm not really sure about that one. Perhaps the real issue is that it should have all been sorted out years ago, peaceably around the conference table, and we caused the invasion by hanging back on that. Positive peace-making does seem to be the important thing – something that we obviously need to pay more attention to. Then there might be less war-making. I suppose that is the difference between peace and that old biblical word 'shalom'. It means more than just the absence of war, it is the positive presence of peace, love and justice.

Well, Auntie Flo, as they say on all the best chat shows, 'that's all we've got time for now', and in keeping with a much greater tradition, I wish you shalom.

God bless you,

Love David

9: Peacemakers

Dear Auntie Flo,

You remember some weeks ago I wrote to you about being persecuted for the faith? I wondered then whether there are things in our society that conflict with our faith and whether we oughtn't to stand up and be counted a bit more, even risking persecution. Well my good friend and compulsive anti-flow person Jill Pritchard must have heard my thoughts.

It all came out of our last house-group meeting. Starting our customary ten minutes late with all of us there except Jill, John Wilson opened with prayers. In the midst of the prayers, he casually mentioned Jill, 'unable to be with us because she is in prison'. The approving murmer of 'mms' and 'Amens' ceased abruptly and, in the pregnant silence, a number of surprised and surreptitious glances passed between us. Meanwhile John ploughed on regardless. His final Amen had hardly left his lips before there was a babble of inquiry. What on earth had she done now, I wondered. Had that bag of hers finally been classified as an offensive weapon?

Apparently John had assumed that we all knew about it as it had been reported in the local paper and that was why he had dropped it in so nonchalently. Jill had been arrested at a demonstration against the building of a nuclear missile base. As soon as John said it, I remembered her saying that she was going off there because she had felt that Christians ought to be represented at such protests. 'Nuclear weapons are immoral', she had said, and in one of her characteristically sweeping statements, 'no Christian can support the possession of them and it's time we stood up to be counted.' She obviously had stood up and been counted – at least by the police who had arrested her for trespassing and refusing to keep the peace.

You can imagine the discussion that followed! First of all we had a rather polarised discussion about 'not matter what the cause you cannot break the law!' It was interesting to see that those who supported that one and condemned Jill's action tend to be the same people who approved of Christians in Russia who have broken Russian law. It would seem that it's all right to break other countries' laws, particularly if they are communist. Anyway we soon left that subject and got on to the real nitty-gritty of nuclear disarmament.

John Wilson said, 'Well, it's all in a good cause', as a sort of passing remark in the hope I think of closing the discussion and moving on to what he had prepared for the meeting, but he wasn't allowed to get away with that.

'But is it?' piped up my worthy landlord Sandy Prime. 'I think these anti-nuclear demonstrators are talking a lot of very dangerous rubbish!'

Second pregnant pause of the evening.

Amy coughed and I said, 'But surely you can't support the use of nuclear arms? I'm not a pacifist,' I continued, surprised at my own new-found assurance in that area, 'but nuclear arms are a very different thing. They're so indiscriminate, for one thing, you can't hit just economic targets or even just soldiers, but everybody gets it and keeps on getting it for years to come with all that radioactive fall-out.'

'Yes OK,' said Sandy, 'the use of nuclear arms would be terrible, but we're not talking about that. We are talking about the possession of nuclear arms. You see it's the threat of use that counts. We have got to deter the Russians from invading, by threatening them with something sufficiently terrible. Conventional weapons, guns and tanks and that sort of thing would not deter them because they – and you, it would seem – find the damage they inflict acceptable.'

Sly dig at me there I thought, but he carried on.

'Sure I would never want to see nuclear weapons used', he said, 'but that is the very reason we need them, because the Russians wouldn't want them used either.

They know that as soon as they try to devastate us, we can devastate them so it's a stalemate. But it's a stalemate that works. It has kept peace in Europe for nearly forty years.'

With that, he relaxed back from the edge of his chair and sat with a defiant look on his face. Let it be known, Sandy Prime has strong views on this subject!

'I think it's madness,' said one of the others. 'Just think of all the money that's being spent on it.'

'Yes,' said Sandy, quickly back on the edge of his chair. 'But all that money means jobs for people here in Britain. If you demolished the armaments industry there would be a lot more unemployment than we have already.'

'But surely,' said John, 'you can't support nuclear arms on that basis? That money could be spent on other more useful things – to help the appalling poverty in the world, for example. The factories could be converted to other types of work. In fact, I know that some unions in these factories have already proposed alternative projects that they could work on.'

I thought I would get back into the discussion and said, 'If nothing else, surely the over-kill, the fact that the Americans and the Russians can destroy each other hundreds of times over, must be absurd.'

'Of course it is,' said Sandy. 'That's why we have all these talks about limitations and reductions. The Americans do want to reduce the weapons they have but that has got to be balanced by a similar reduction from the Russians. This is where the big difference is with these anti-nuclear campaigns. The Americans are willing to reduce on a multilateral basis, which means all those involved doing it together. But these campaigners are talking about unilateral disarmament; they say that we ought to get rid of all our nuclear weapons and throw the American missiles out of Britain, without seeking any reductions from the Russians. Now that is far more likely to cause war than to stop it because once the stability of the present peace is unbalanced, then the Russians will be more likely to invade. In a perfect world we wouldn't need arms, but David, you are the one who talks about the lesser of two evils in a fallen world. Isn't the possession of nuclear arms as a deterrent less of an evil than war with Russia?'

Well I must admit that I could see what Sandy meant and I was going to ask him more about it but just at that moment the door bell rang. Amy went off to answer it and then let out a squeal of delight. Who should be there but our long-lost sister, Jill!

'Come in,' said John. 'Welcome back! We have just been talking about you. Or, at least, you had prompted our discussion!'

There followed a time of general hilarity, with jokes about jail-birds, and 'it's sure been quiet round here' and so on. But once Jill had her mug of coffee clasped in her hand, we got back down to the real business.

Being my normal naîve self, I re-launched the discussion by saying how we had been discussing nuclear arms and that I could see that supporting unilateral disarmament could have a serious destabilising effect on the precariously balanced peace. I asked Jill whether she didn't feel it more likely to cause war than to prevent it? As I spoke, I quickly realised that I had managed in the way only I can, to draw the fire from Sandy directly to myself! The coffee mug, half-way to her lips, never made it and she launched into one of her best streams of invective yet. It seems that I am typical of all these 'two-faced war mongerers' who talk about peace while preparing for war, who talk about the need to trust each other while scaremongering and deceiving at every possible opportunity. (She's got a wonderful turn of phrase!)

'The 1970s were a UN Decade of Disarmament' she said, 'and even though everybody expressed the will to disarm – it was only if the "others" would – hardly anything happened. The years since that decade have been almost as bad. The great powers talk and talk about disarmament, but the big question remains: do they really have the will to disarm? If everybody recognises that it is madness to be able to kill each other so many times over, then why haven't they been progressively disarming? I don't believe they really do want to disarm; they are too eaten up with their own fears of each other.'

Jill paused there and I thought I might be able to explain that I had only been thinking aloud about something Sandy has said, but I had no chance. As soon as I opened my mouth, she started again.

'And don't forget the armaments industry. It is a very strong lobby in the United States and any government is ultimately looking at its votes, not moral niceties. You see,' she continued, 'the people who are in power are basically concerned with keeping that power, both over other countries and over their own people. They protect their power over other countries by nuclear weapons and over their own people by saying that they really do want to disarm but only multilaterally. They apparently make attempts to disarm or at least reduce arms, but I am sure those are really only show-pieces to keep their own people happy. The argument about multilateralism versus unilateralism is a big red herring. There is a saying that "a unilateralist is a multilateralist who means business". I want to disarm and I mean it so much that I am willing for us to disarm first.'

Sandy wasn't as polite as I was and dived in at this point with his second claim for the evening that this was all rubbish – dangerous rubbish at that. 'You seem to forget the fact that Russia wants to take over the world,' he said. 'If we disarm, it is an open invitation for Russia to invade us, especially if all your lunatic friends on the continent persuade their governments to do the same.'

You'll notice we're very honest with each other in our discussions – well, that's one way of putting it!

'Who says they want to take over the world?' returned Jill, ignoring the slur on her sanity. 'That's what I mean by scaremongering. Yes, Russia has surrounded herself with a ring of "friendly states", but some believe that she has good cause to be concerned after all she has been through – including 20 million people killed in the Second World War.

'And yes,' Jill continued, 'Russia did invade Afghanistan – though some would say, while agreeing it was wrong, that she was simply propping up an ailing communist country. But really I can't believe that the Russian people have any desire for another war. What advantage would it be to Russia to invade Britain? She has enough trouble surviving as it is. The only point would be to wipe out the American and British nuclear weapons that threaten her safety. If we disarmed, there wouldn't be any weapons here to threaten her. This is the great problem with the present state of stability: it is based on fear.

'That fear causes mistrust, which helps fuel the continuing "cold war" mentality and influences Russian and American involvement, however disguised, in places like Africa and Latin America. And,' she delivered her final shot, 'don't forget Vietnam – America's war – when we talk about Russia's Afghanistan.'

While Jill was pouring out this lengthy and at times colourful diatribe I suddenly remembered that word 'shalom' and all the discussions I told you about in my last letter. Here too is the need for positive peace-making. Peace is not just an absence of war but also an absence of the very sort of mistrust that Jill was talking about. I raised this, when I could get a word in edgeways, and was greeted like a long-lost friend.

'That's it,' said Jill. 'We have got to make peace possible. The experiences of the past thirty or so years show that you can't do that while holding nuclear missiles at each other's throats – even if you don't use them. We have not had peace for thirty-seven years, merely an absence of war.

'The policy of the nuclear deterrent,' she continued, 'has not worked in creating peace in the Christian sense of that word. It is the world's way of working, not God's. Surely Jesus teaches us that the Christian way is a way of sacrifice and reconciliation? And that must mean being willing to give up your arms (even if you do it alone at first) to sacrifice your sense of security and to be willing to work for the understanding that will create real peace? Nobody can say for certain that a Russian threat does not exist, though there are reasons to suggest that it is unlikely; disarming in the face of that is the sacrifice that could make peace possible. Much work would have to be done on healing the wounds of fear but the call to discipleship was never shown to be easy.'

Jill obviously sensed that she might be getting somewhere with us and had begun to slow her pace down! Sandy was looking very sceptical and when prompted by John could only say that it was all so unrealistic. 'It is all very well bringing God into it to try and lend some weight to your argument, but you have to face the fact that we live in a fallen-world.'

John said, 'Isn't that the very fact that makes the sacrifice necessary?'

Amy joined in at this point with a different issue: 'If Jill is right and the powerful have no will to disarm and indeed intend to keep the situation as it is, in order to maintain power, then what is the point of demonstrations?'

Jill exclaimed, as is her habit, and said that she had been reading something about that just recently. She dived into her bag and somehow managed to find a piece of paper which she smoothed out on her knee. 'This is a quote from a guy called Boukousky who is a Russian dissident living in England. He said "it is not the gun, it is not the tanks, nor the atomic bomb, which give power; power does not rest on them. Power is born of the docility of man, from acceptance of authority, from obedience." We can't just go on passively accepting what has gone on for the last four decades: we have got to stand up and say something, even do something, I think that is the right Christian response – even if it does mean getting put in prison.'

Well, I suppose that brought us right back to the beginning. However, it also brought us more or less to the end as we had been at it most of the evening by that stage and John had long since abandoned any hope of bringing us round to the official topic for the evening.

I had gone to John and Amy's with Sandy and Diane,

so we had a rather strained drive home! When I got back to the flat I sat for some time before going to bed trying to think it through. What really stood out in my mind was Jill saying that the policy of nuclear deterrence was not God's way and that it had brought no 'shalom', no positive sense of love and justice. I think that clinched it for me. Giving up your arms seems folly in the eyes of the world but surely that's the very essence of anti-flow? We don't look to the world. We look to God.

Well, there it is, Auntie Flo, yet another evening in the life of our house-group. It's nothing if not eventful! And it certainly makes you think.

Look after yourself, and let the crowd know I'm still alive and waiting patiently for all the letters they promised!

Love to you,

God bless,

David

10: Work but no job

Dear Auntie Flo,

Our house group continues to flourish. I think I told you that we have a session at each meeting when we can talk about things that are on our mind. It is a great way of becoming closer to each other and sharing burdens and joys, either practically or in prayer. At our meeting last night we had just such a session and it turned out to be very interesting.

The story really starts months ago, before I joined, when one of the group, Phil, was made redundant from his job in a warehouse. It was a great shock to him. I think you either assume redundancy will never happen to you or live under constant dread of it. Phil was one of the former, so apparently he took it quite hard. I can remember the first meeting I went to when Phil explained how he felt rejected by the world. He had applied for lots of jobs and had never been successful, not even as much as an interview – in fact, not even a reply from some places. He is only about the same age as me but really felt that he was finished, 'worthless' as he put it.

Well, we prayed a lot for Phil that night and at other meetings and got quite concerned because he had not been seen for several weeks. But last night he turned up again at our house group, and what a change there was in him. You could tell as soon as he came in. There was a smile on his face and he even cracked a few jokes with John Wilson about his newly acquired beard. Thank God for answered prayer, I thought, he has got a job at last. Someone asked him with great expectancy about how the job search was going. We were all surprised when Phil said that he still had not found one! Gulp and acute embarrassment all round. He apologised for not having

REDUNDANT

been about for a while and said that he had been rather busy.

John couldn't contain himself any longer and said, 'Come on, out with it! What have you been up to?' Rather bold, I thought, but you could see that Phil was loving every minute of it, keeping us in suspense!

'Oh, this and that,' he said, at which point John hurled cushions at him and threatened him with a stool, so Phil told all.

Apparently on a visit to the park one day, trying to fill his empty hours, he sat on a bench near a group of lads playing football. After a kick-around the lads were trying to make up a couple of teams for a match but found they had odd numbers. An older guy with the group came over and asked Phil if he fancied a game. Phil, one-time reserve for the school 'D' team, thought he might as well rediscover his talent and joined in. The match ended with Phil wondering how he even managed the 'D' team but nevertheless the happier for his social (or rather, physical) contact with the outside world. The lads wandered off and as the older chap thanked Phil they struck up a conversation. It turned out that he was a youth worker; he was attached to a local youth club but had a particular responsibility for working with young people who belonged to no clubs, most of whom were out of work. Phil and Ron formed quite a friendship and met each other a number of times either at the park or at a particular café down in Brice. It was on one of these occasions that Ron asked Phil if he would come along with him as a helper on a weekend trip he was organising for some of the kids. Phil took his courage (and his sleeping-bag) in both hands and agreed to go. Apparently they had a tremendous time even though he didn't have much time to use the sleeping-bag!

Since then (after catching up on his sleep) Phil has been spending a lot of time working with Ron and various groups of these unemployed young people. It is purely voluntary, he says, but at last he has found something that shows that he is not worthless. Here is something he can do, he enjoys doing it and feels that he is making some contribution to society. Ron and the kids value him, even if no one else does. He said: 'I was quite amazed by all this because Ron was the last person I would imagine as a youth worker. Humping boxes yes, but not bending a listening ear to some lad in distress. Just shows you, I suppose.'

We spent a lot of time that evening talking about unemployment and work. Phil was saying that our normal reaction to the problem of unemployment is that we want to see more jobs created, more factories opened up or at least fewer shut down and so on. But the facts are that we do not need so many people now to create the same amount of wealth. In that sense, the jobs, though not the people, *are* redundant. Not only that but we shouldn't really want to re-create some of the jobs that lots of people have had to do. Many were boring, repetitive and dirty.

'It's all very well saying that, but until recently you would have been glad of any job, just like thousands of others,' someone said.

'That's right,' said Phil, 'but let's think about why that was. When I left work I lost a lot of my friends, I hardly ever saw them after that and had few people to talk to during the day. With very little to do, I lost the routine that work gives you. You can only do so much wallpapering at home. I also lost the status that the job gave me. You know, when you get introduced to people they say 'This is Phil and he's a . . .', then they get embarrassed because you're not anything – you're at the bottom of the pile. I also lost the money from the job – that also means a drop in status because you can't buy the things you did before and you're dependent upon charity – the dole – to get money to live. Now I think we ought to be looking at different ways of giving these things to people, instead of talking about getting back to full employment. That's just a political gambit spread by governments that can't look past the next election.'

Our Phil seems to have had a slight touch of political

education from this youth worker, I thought – 'political gambits' no less. His self-confidence really seems to have taken a boost, even more so than when he was at the warehouse. Sandy Prime seemed to have the same idea about Phil's politicisation and asked him who this youth worker was. 'Does he have a hammer and sickle on his jeans?' he asked.

At this point Phil got rather upset to say the least. 'That's just typical of you lot,' he said. 'Everything is in little boxes and you can't imagine anything outside of that. Just because he thinks a bit and talks about politics, doesn't mean he's a raving communist. In fact he's a Christian, he goes to St Chads.' So, take that folks, we had obviously touched on a rather sore point and Sandy apologised. Phil relaxed and accepted the apology. It was just that he had been going through a bit of a rough time, he explained, and Ron had been the only person to really help him see his way through it, and now we had started knocking him. OK, point taken, but surely we had tried to help him out too?

'Yes,' said Phil, 'but only in terms of getting a *job*. You prayed that I might get a job and even helped me get an interview, but don't you see that the whole thing is much deeper than that, it needs a much more radical approach.'

Oh dear, I thought, I've heard that word 'radical' somewhere before: anti-flow rides again.

'There simply are not enough jobs to go round,' he continued. 'If I get one because of your help it simply means that someone else goes without. People are obsessed with "jobs" rather than "work", and are more concerned to get out of the present crisis back to where we were, than to see the opportunities in this situation to create a new and better understanding of people and their work. Some of the jobs that people had to do were terrible and we are all trapped by the status linked to the job we do and the money we get. Surely that can't be a very Christian view of life? We should be working against that view, not going along with it. I haven't got a job to do, but I've found plenty of work with Ron and the kids. I've found new friends, I've got some sort of routine and I can tell you that I feel much more fulfilled than I did with my last job. I'm really enjoying it, I have found something I seem to be quite good at, it's much more worthwhile than the work I was doing in the warehouse and I feel as if I am really helping people. The only things missing are 'status' – in the eyes of society to them I'm still unemployed and a scrounger – and money; I still have to depend on charity, and very little of it at that. But don't you think we ought, as Christians, to be challenging that sort of approach, instead of just trying our best to get people back into "jobs" no matter what they are and what they do to people?'

Well, that rather floored everybody. A real anti-flow approach if ever I saw one, and I could understand what he meant. Valuing people for what they are and not simply what they do. I suppose the new technology we are always hearing about is bound to mean that we need fewer people to create the necessary wealth. The question is, what do we do with all those people who are being told that they are not needed? I suppose this time of change is a real opportunity for Christians to seek an adjustment in the way we value people and their contribution to society. They are not just 'units of production' but individuals with needs and hopes that can probably be fulfilled in better ways than in the old system of work. Some of us do enjoy our work and are fulfilled by it, but many do not and have to gain that fulfilment outside their jobs. Phil said that we ought to value people because of their contribution to society whether that is producing things to create wealth, looking after old ladies or keeping pigeons. They are all 'useful' and none should be more highly valued than others or given more money. We should get our money because we are people, not because we happen to do a job as a factory hand or a social worker.

Sandy Prime rather reacted against all this 'communist nonsense' as he called it. 'It would mean a complete restructuring of society, a complete change in the way we operate.'

But Phil said, 'That's right – and isn't that what Jesus called us to?' I suppose there is no answer to that.

Sandy was not satisfied, though. 'What about all the people who are unemployed now?' he said. 'You're talking about something that means a complete change in people's attitudes, which you are simply not likely to get. You ask most unemployed people what they want: they want jobs, not fancy theorising about what life could be like. We might like a change, but frankly it is just not on.'

John Wilson stepped in at this point and said that he agreed with Sandy but . . . A great one for 'Yes . . . but's, is our John! 'It is unlikely that we are going to get society to change its views completely about work and the value of people but shouldn't we as Christians be grasping the opportunity now that people are thinking about work to get them at least to consider this sort of viewpoint? Whatever does eventually happen could come a little more in line with this view of people if we make a stand and don't just invest everything in the old view of work. We can't give up simply because it seems a lost cause. 'Where's your faith?' he said. 'With all these new government-training courses, especially for young people, we ought to be pressing for them to be helped to develop as individuals, able to seek out opportunities and meet their own needs, not just to be trained as more 'workmen'. Let's face it, many of them are not going to get work for a good few years yet, whatever happens.'

Jill Pritchard, our lady of the Sri Lankan sewing-machines and W.D.M. tea, jumped in to say that we surely ought also to be looking at the question of distribution of wealth. 'It can't be right,' she said, 'that some people get such high wages when others are comparatively living on the bread-line just because they are unemployed through no fault of their own.'

Well, Phil certainly set us thinking. I suppose I have been very lucky really. I've always had a job and I have even felt fairly fulfilled, but he certainly opened my eyes to see how important it is to feel wanted or to be making a contribution, and how difficult it is for those who don't have a job. I can also see what he says about how we really only value people in general for what they do and not what they are. I suppose the way in which Jesus valued everybody, even those that no one else would talk to, condemns that sort of view and therefore we ought to stand against it too. Apart from changing the education system, I'm not sure how we can do anything about it, mind. Still, the house group should at least be aware of the question mark now and I suppose that is what attitude changing is all about.

Well, Auntie Flo, I have gone on for long enough. I don't seem to have heard from you for a while. I hope you're OK. I look forward to hearing all the news.

Lots of love,

David

11: Just a mother

Dear Auntie Flo,

I'm sorry I have not been in touch for a few weeks but I hope you feel honoured reading this letter now it has arrived! I am actually writing it at 7.30 in the morning. Which, I can tell you, for me is some great feat. I hope there are not too many spelling mistakes. I'm not sure if my brain works at this time of day. I seem to have been out such a lot lately, what with various meetings and invitations to dinner. Alongside all that, I have been trying to get the flat into a final state of order. I have now got a few posters on the wall, some light-shades up and even a shelf or two. So I thought I had better make an early start this morning and write to you before I go to work. Anyway, thanks for your letter, I'm glad that the leg is not too bad.

I know what you mean about jobs: people do simply want employment; they are not interested in changing attitudes, theirs or anyone else's. But I think we must somehow come to terms with the important issues that Phil raised. You know as well as I do that there is lots to do in the community, people to be looked after, things to be built, places to be tidied up – which seems silly when there are so many unemployed. But I am sure that the answer is not just to get back to employment as we knew it. It will be a tremendous waste of an opportunity if that is all that happens. It is our attitudes to work and employment that need to change.

We had a very good example of this last night. I was at John and Amy's for supper and Amy told us about a form that she had to fill in at the bank. The assistant asked her whether she 'worked', so Amy said, 'Yes, I'm a housewife and mother.'

The girl said, 'But have you got a job?'

'Yes,' said Amy, 'that's a job, isn't it?'

The girl wouldn't have it, though, and just put a line through that box.

Now Amy is not exactly your militant feminist, no chaining herself to the railings or anything like that, but I could tell that this had rather hit home, and it led to a very interesting conversation. I suppose it is a classic case of an occupation being undervalued because it is not recognised as a job. A housewife and/or mother doesn't technically get paid for her work, so is she assumed to do it for the love of it? She does a lot of it inside the house, there is no fixed time given over to it (apart from twenty-four hours a day, that is!) and it is not reckoned to require any specialist training. Because of our attitudes to employment and status, this work has therefore been devalued and given less status than any other profession. You even hear women introducing themselves with, 'I'm just a housewife' or 'I'm just a mother'. It is quite amazing when you think about it, isn't it? I mean, there can't really be any more important a job than bringing up children and yet some women, perhaps most even, have been forced into seeing themselves as less important than an office worker.

Amy was saying she felt that this attitude had a lot to do with the whole feminist movement. Many women support it or versions of it, not particularly because they want to go out and get jobs, but because they want to be recognised for the contribution that they already make to society in the home. 'Obviously,' Amy said, 'it is important that women should get equal opportunities to develop in whatever profession they wish but the most important fact is that they should gain the worth they already deserve in society's eyes, and which they do not have because we devalue, at least subconsciously, the work they do.

Amy was saying that she had been looking at some of the classic passages in Corinthians (1 Cor. 11 and 14) and Timothy (1 Tim. 2) where Paul makes his main comments on the role of women. Now Paul is reckoned by many to be the original male chauvinist but Amy was saying that Paul was actually speaking out to protect the role and status of women in society. Apparently there were many pagan practices in the city of Corinth at the time that abused and devalued women. Relationships between men and women that honoured God and respected the worth of each were disintegrating.

Paul was striving to protect the church from these influences and to bring order back into their worship. Now I suppose one could say the very same things about us today. Women have been and are continuously devalued in our society (just look at advertising!) and that affects the relationships between the sexes. Now if Christianity is about anything then I suppose it is about right relationships. Not only between people and God, but also between people themselves. Paul was trying to point out what relationships should be like between men and women, to support the place of women and to restore respect for them and their role. His comments seem to have been directed both to men and women. He was reminding women that they didn't do their own cause any good if they behaved inappropriately in church, according to the customs of the day. (That would make men respect them even less.) At the same time he was reminding men that they were less than complete without women, otherwise God would not have needed to create women. There are many roles that are interchangeable between men and women but in other ways they are each unique, and that uniqueness should not be denied.

'Right,' I said, 'I can take that, but the great question is of course, what are the things that are unique to men or to women?'

Amy conceded that this is the contentious issue. It is not clear, apart from the biological differences, as to what the uniqueness of each is. And she reckoned that it wasn't clear from the Bible either, as to what were the basic principles and what were factors relating to the traditions and culture of that day. Ordination of women is the big question for the Anglicans I suppose. But how much is what Paul says on that to do with culture and how much to do with basic principles? A good question.

So as not to be left out, John raised the issue of headship! Isn't Paul quite clear in stating that man is the head and women come second? Well, much to the annoyance I'm sure of all real feminists, Amy agreed. But she said that that has to be seen in the context of man under the headship of God. Man can't lord it over woman as much as he likes because she has a positive and unique role just as he has, both under the headship of God.

'If you agree with that,' I said, 'then doesn't that definitely cut women out from being ordained?' Got her there, I thought. But she said that if we believe in the priesthood of all believers and that Christian ministry is not about rank, authority and status but about being servants, then surely it does not cut women out! *Touché*!

Well we prattled on for ages about that. It was very interesting. I'd never thought about it before, but I found this thing about women not being valued for the work that they do in the house and bringing up children to be fascinating. It's quite horrific when you think about it. I mean all the attitudes and values that we have start off in our childhood. I know that friends and school have a big effect but the home must be where a lot of the groundwork is done. So the work of a mother who, I suppose, is the principal child-rearer in most cases, is absolutely vital in the development of society.

So many of the problems and issues that we deal with are greatly affected by attitudes, and those attitudes are formed in early childhood. This anti-flow thing is all about attitudes as well. The home, and therefore the mother in particular, must play at least some part in deciding whether, as Christians in later life, we take our guidance from society or from a more radical view of our Christian faith.

I thought back to that talk that we had with Mr Asago about violence. Remember, I wrote to you about it a few weeks ago. He stressed that the answer to doing away with wars was the development of the desire for peace-making. That desire must be a key thing for mothers to be teaching, and that very positive role as teachers should be recognised. I suppose that if children don't learn to settle their differences peaceably (to give and to take) at that age, then there is little hope of them doing it when they are older.

Well, it was a fascinating dinner, I can tell you. It gave me a whole new understanding about women and the feminist movement. Mind you, I think it was going against the flow of some of the feminist arguments as much as it was anti-flow society's undervaluing view of women. Thinking about it now, I realise it didn't deal with the fact that some men recognise the valuable work of women in the home but also reckon that they should stay there! But going out to work can't, I'm sure, be seen as part of man's uniqueness. Anyway, whatever it missed out, I don't think I will take women for granted as much now as I did. Well, I'll try not to anyway!

I must go or I am going to be late for work. As it is I will have to go in the car instead of by bus – well that's my excuse, anyway. The wonderful machine cost me nearly £60 for new tyres the other day. Such are the joys of mobility. Well I'd better go and hope the thing starts.

Lots of love to you and the crowd. Do give my congratulations to the Watsons on their new arrival.

God bless,

Love David

12: A white problem

Dear Auntie Flo,

Here I am again! Life goes on as ever but, I must admit, with a certain amount of excitement this week. Or perhaps fear might be a more appropriate description.

After our discussion about work with Phil the other week, I had a chat with him about this youth work he has been doing. He said that if I was interested he would take me down to Brice to meet Ron (that's the youth worker) and to have a look around. So – as always – a glutton for punishment, I agreed and we arranged to go down there last Tuesday evening. Phil and I went down in my car and met Ron at a run-down empty shop which he shares as a sort of base with a number of other organisations including a legal-advice centre. I must admit, in the back of my mind I suppose I had expected Ron to be an intense, bearded, hairy young activist. So I was rather taken aback when he turned out to be an admittedly rather dishevelled but otherwise clean-shaven, quietly spoken, ordinary looking guy in his mid-thirties. Now I know that's not old but all these things are relative, you must admit! We talked a bit about the area of Brice. Ron explained how it is made up of fairly old housing in what was once the relatively rich end of town. As the rich moved out the large houses were broken up into flats and rented off or just allowed to run down. A large population of people of West Indian origin are buying up the housing and in some places restoring it to its former glory. It has, however, the reputation of being a rough area with a relatively high crime rate, a lot of unemployment, and various other problems, some of which are associated with the tensions between blacks and whites in society. I nodded sagely at this point, failing to really understand

its significance, little guessing that my eyes were about to be opened! After a cup of coffee – correction a large mug of coffee – Ron offered to take us out and show me round. I readily agreed, much as I would if someone offered to show me round their back garden or new house. I very quickly realised that if you are really going to find out about people, it is not so easy just to be an on-looker, without getting involved.

We wandered off out of the shop and up the road. We saw the housing, some of it in a pretty bad state, but some of it also looking quite good. We saw the people on the streets and Ron said hello to a few. It was getting quite dark by this stage, but Ron noticed a couple of black lads in the light of a shop window, further along on the opposite side of the street. He recognised them as two good contacts of his and suggested we went over for a chat. Just at that moment a police car sped along the road, stopped just ahead of the boys and two policemen jumped out and started talking to them.

From where we were standing the policemen seemed to push the two lads in against the wall and obviously some rather intense discussion was going on. Ron told us to hang on a minute and went over to the group. Meanwhile I felt rather disconcerted by the whole thing. The lads had simply been walking along the road, one with a plastic carrier bag, not – at least not obviously – up to anything. But they had been stopped by the police. Obviously they must be 'known to the police' as they say, and perhaps there had been some theiving or 'suspicious activity'. However, the whole thing took an even more bizarre turn when Ron joined them: he too was pushed against the wall in none too gentle a fashion by one of the policemen who proceeded to give him a good talking 'at' with a finger prodding his shoulder. The other policeman meanwhile was going through the carrier bag. After a few more minutes the police went back to their car and started up. They drove past very slowly – giving us a rather intense look as they went by. Ron was chatting to the two lads and we went over to find out what had happened. Apparently, far from being 'known to the police', the two lads had been in no trouble and in fact were just on their way to a Bible study group at the local Pentecostal church. Ron knew them because of their links there. The mysterious carrier bag actually held one lad's Bible and a radio he had recently received as a present which he was taking to show off at church.

I put my foot in it at once by saying that I supposed that the high crime rate had something to do with the police having to keep a look-out for suspicious goings-on. At which Ron nearly erupted! 'What's suspicious about simply walking down the street?' he said. 'And why are the black kids the ones that get stopped?'

'Yes, and why do they treat us like dirt?' one of the lads joined in. 'They swear at us, push us around and accuse us of all sorts of things, a lot of it is simply because we are black and young. This isn't the first time you know – it's always happening.'

The whole thing was horrific. You could feel his hatred just as you could see it in the way the police had dealt with them. Two parts of society hating each other. I asked Ron what the police had said to him and apparently they had accused him of being a 'nigger lover' and told him that if he interfered he would be arrested for 'obstructing a police officer in the course of his duty'. It was amazing. I can still feel the fear when the policeman stared at Phil and me when they drove past – it made me physically shrink back into the wall. There must be something wrong here, I thought.

We said good-night to the lads and made our way back to the old shop. 'What on earth is it all about?' I asked Ron. I don't know about you, Auntie Flo, but I've heard stories about this sort of thing but never really believed that it happens – well not to any extent anyway. The occasional bad apple is a fact of life, even in the police force. They do, after all, have a very difficult and necessary job to do, so there is bound to be a bit of tension. But when good law-abiding citizens are harassed then there must be something wrong.

'Well,' said Ron, as he opened the door and went to put the kettle on. 'It's two things really. First there is the fact that we are really at a turning point in society. The move to a post-industrial society and the change in the work pattern mean there are inevitably certain tensions and problems at the moment while things get sorted out.' I thought back to our discussion with Phil and I could see what he was meaning there. He went on to say that when there is any problem or tension within society it is usually the poor that come off the worst. It means that if there is a shortage of housing then everyone comes down a rung, that forces prices up and it is the poor who fall off the bottom. Same with jobs – the skilled take less skilled jobs and the least skilled miss out. So at some stage the poor and disadvantaged are bound to become discontented and some will hit back. The rich majority in society then demand that the government exert control. They usually do that through the police force. So the police get caught at the painful meeting points where the tension often erupts. Theirs is a very difficult and tense job and many police are frustrated by that. Some of them take that frustration out on the public.

Well I could see what he was saying but it seemed to be giving a free hand for people to do just what they want and I said so. Some people need little excuse, especially in areas like Brice, to make as much trouble as they can. Well I seemed to be making a good job of saying all the wrong things to Ron. He had another little eruption.

'That is a typical white middle-class racist attitude. Yes, there are some pure criminals in Brice who need to be caught, but what is going on around them has an awful lot to do with people's responses. What about all the fiddles that white middle-class businessmen pull to make sure they keep near the top of the pile? Tax avoidance, evasion or whatever you want to call it for a start.'

'Now hang on,' I said. 'I never brought the question of race into it, you did.'

'No,' said Ron. 'You may not have mentioned it but I

am sure it is in your mind right enough. It is there in most of us to a greater or lesser extent. Don't you see, that was the other main factor in the little incident before with the police. If you are young you stand a greater chance of being stopped than if you are middle-aged or old. If you are black then you stand an even greater chance of being stopped and badly treated, and there is no use in you trying to deny that, because that is the experience of black youth today, whether you like it or not. There is evidence of an amount of overt-racism in the police today. But more than that we have to recognise the racism that is in all of us, whether policemen or not. The problem is that if you take into consideration what we said before about the police being at the sharp end of the conflict within society, then there is a greater chance of that racism coming out through making people of other races scapegoats. We can't just blame the police,' said Ron. 'We have got to look at the tensions we are creating within society and how they are made worse by our own racism!'

Phil suggested at that point that it was time we went – before I put my foot in it again, I think. So I thanked Ron for his time and we wandered off back to the car. When we got there the aerial had been broken off and one of the tyres let down! My immediate thought was 'Young BLACK hooligans!' But as soon as I had said it, I realised the conclusion to which I had jumped – 'Black hooligans,' not just hooligans, but black ones. Now I suppose I can excuse myself and say that there are a lot of black people who live in Brice and so it was only natural to think that, but there are lots of white kids around too, so was Ron right? Do we all have a certain suspicion deep down about people of another race?

By the time we had managed to change the wheel (I think Samson must have tightened the wheel nuts up – I had to call on Phil to undo them!) and I had dropped Phil off, I got home rather late and very tired. As I relaxed in the bath I thought back to when I was looking for somewhere to live and remembered my visit to the other end of

Brice. I realised that I had been put off the large flat I had seen there not by the flat itself but by the fact that I would have been surrounded by black neighbours who lived a bit differently to me. Perhaps, in fact, I would have found it more interesting and lively than my present rather quiet and reserved neighbourhood, if I could have got over the initial suspicious thoughts. I thought too of my initial unease with Steve Asago – was that simply unease at his message and his dark glasses or did that hide a deeper unease at his colour?

Something I had been reading in the Bible the night before came to mind and when I got out of the bath I looked it up. It's in Luke 4. When Jesus preaches in the synogogue at Nazareth and is rejected by his own people, he told them to beware of thinking that there is only one people or one nation who has got it right and who enjoy God's grace. He reminded them, for example, that though there were many lepers in Israel, Elisha healed Naamen the Syrian.

Perhaps we British are too self-righteous in thinking that we do things right and everybody else has got it wrong. Like expecting all foreigners to be able to speak English – or at least to understand if you shout! I suppose when people are a different colour as well, that focuses the feelings even more.

One could say that it is only natural, but does that make it right? To be true to anti-flow, the answer must be no. We need to recognise that this hate-racism, a bias against those of other races and towards our own, is there – in all of us – and take steps to see that we don't damage others by ignoring it. The fact that there are these racial problems and that there are proportionately far more black people in poor housing or without jobs than white people, would seem to indicate that we have not recognised and compensated for our 'natural' racism. I certainly didn't like being called a racist by Ron but perhaps I am – perhaps we all are and we ought to admit it, instead of hotly denying that we are and blaming black people for something that is our problem.

Well, Auntie Flo, what do you think? Are you a racist? You spent a lot of time with people of a different race when you were out in India. Do you think that helped you work through your feelings about people of another race or did it make you worse?

Well, I had better be going – it's house group tonight. Perhaps I'll tell them they are all racists! That'll put the cat among the pigeons! Sandy Prime has got Scottish blood in him; will that mean he agrees that we are all racists or will he say it's a Sassenachs-only problem? I don't know, but I'm sure he'll have something to say about it!

Look after yourself,

God bless you,

Love David

13: The bottom line

Dear Auntie Flo,

Thanks for your letter and your comments. Yes, I do realise that it is important to be proud of your country, or of your church or family for that matter, and I suppose there is nothing wrong with that. The problem is that it can (and does) so easily get out of hand. Pride can turn to excessive nationalism or chauvinism. I suppose it's the same with the male chauvinism thing. Being proud to be a man is OK until it means you look down on women or devalue them. I mean, I'm proud to support my football club (even though they do lose half the time) but I don't take to beating up supporters of other clubs which is what it can lead to. I remember you saying once before that, when you were a missionary, there was always the danger of thinking that it is not only our religion that is right but our culture as well. This blind cultural chauvinism means that the native cultural heritage is ignored and discarded.

Anyway, you may be amazed to hear that I have been back to see Ron since I last wrote. I did find it a rather painful experience the first time, but I have gradually come to feel sure that there is a lot there that I have to come to terms with if I really do believe all this anti-flow stuff. Jesus did associate with those rejected by society and say that he had been chosen 'to bring the good news to the poor'. What is our response to be to the rejected and poor of our society? Those people who live in places like Brice and get the thin end of the wedge just because they are poor.

So I thought I would go and have another chat with Ron. I must say I think he was almost as surprised to see me back as I was to find myself there. But I asked him what he as a Christian thought we ought to be doing

about these sorts of problems. I said I had thought about trying to get our church to sponsor some sort of project in Brice. Perhaps a youth club or a centre where people could meet. 'I have heard that you can get money from the government for that sort of thing,' I said, 'I thought that with that and some money raised at the church and perhaps I could get my insurance brokers to put a bit in, we could employ some people and equip some sort of centre.' Ron snorted – I really seem to manage to put my foot in it every time I open my mouth with that guy. I don't know why I bother.

'Yes,' he says, 'you could do that and you could sponsor a government-training scheme for young people while you're at it.' That's a good idea, I thought, failing at first to catch the sarcasm. 'But what difference is it going to make?' he said. 'Once you've trained the kids and increased their expectations, they are still going to go back on the dole because there are no jobs even if they are trained, especially if they are black. You may set up a club but what are you trying to do, keep them occupied and contain their frustrations?'

'Well,' I said, 'that can't be a bad thing. What do you expect, given that we can't change the world?'

'OK,' he said, 'Perhaps I was a bit harsh, but you must understand my scepticism as I've seen so many good intentions – projects set up by kindly folks who feel they can then forget these people and their problems because they have done their bit. Like giving money to overseas charities – to salve your conscience. You say we can't change the world, but isn't that what Jesus called us to do? Isn't that what the kingdom of God is about? A changed world, people coming back into a right relationship with each other and with God?' I had heard all this somewhere before.

'We have got to change people as well as "problems",' said Ron. 'In many cases people are the problems. Somehow we have got to make the people at your church get to know the people down here in Brice. To identify with them, to listen to them, to hear and understand their problems and to break down racial and social stereo types. Then we might begin to change attitudes on both sides. You don't do that simply by getting money to set up a project. If you employ people to do the work for you, the church members will just leave them to do it and still never come into contact with the people of Brice. No, if they really want to help, then it means their costly involvement as individuals – not just through their pockets. Attitudes and feelings about each other have to be changed and in that way the barriers can be broken down. I am not saying that full-time youth workers or social workers are no good, I'm just saying that they are only a very small part of the solution. You have got to get involved.'

Well there it is. Good old anti-flow again. I told Ron about this anti-flow concept that I had heard about. I can see that he was warning against jumping to the all-too-common conclusion that with enough money and a few bright ideas we can put things right. The solution lies much deeper than that and is much more radical (good anti-flow word!). People have got to be changed as well.

Ron agreed with the anti-flow principles, but said, 'Don't jump to the favourite conclusion that all we have to do then is convert everyone to Christianity and then we will be OK. It is not as simple as that either. Christians can still make mistakes and support systems that create poverty and injustice. South Africa, a supposedly very Christian country, shows that. We have got to bring people into contact with God, but also into contact with each other, so that with God's help they can learn from each other and together work against poverty and injustice. Contact with other people outside of our normal social and religious cliques can help us see those things that we have taken for granted and yet are causing harm to others.'

I've since thought quite hard about that area, well what I mean is I've wrestled with it for hours, nights even. I was going to say that getting people to mix outside their normal social group is just not natural is it? But there I fall immediately into my own trap. Anti-flow doesn't call us just to be 'natural' – it's too easy to be naturally sinful! But you can see what I mean, can't you? The things I enjoy doing, the people in Brice wouldn't enjoy doing and vice versa – would they . . . or would they? I don't know any more – but perhaps that's the point, I don't know what they enjoy. But still, you can't pretend to be what you aren't. I must admit, Ron did say that he didn't think the answer was for everyone to come and live in Brice. (Sandy and Diane Prime will be pleased to hear that!) He said that people had to be genuine, but that means also being genuinely interested in finding out what other people think, in listening, in having contact in some sort of way.

'It's time,' I said to him. 'The problem is that we are all so busy, there are so many things to do in the church, so many things to go to. How can we get involved?'

'That's true,' said Ron, 'but it's not really a question of time but of priorities. There are already too many things for us to go to so we choose between them, don't we? What you are saying to me is that you rate this contact, sharing, listening, working, as a lower priority than all the other things you do.'

Well I suppose that's the bottom line really. It all ends up with what we think is the most important. For most of us – certainly for me – it is all too easy to stick with the things we know. I can think back to when I was choosing somewhere to live. I wanted to find a nice area, somewhere I would feel at home. I wasn't going to mix with people of a totally different culture in Brice. I looked for a church too that I thought was 'sound'. (Mind you, if I had realised it was going to lead me into all this anti-flow, I probably wouldn't have touched it with a barge pole!)

Not only that, but thinking about it just now, I realise that I was so concerned to keep to the safe and familiar thing that I have passed up some great evangelistic opportunities. Do you remember Jim, Mrs Greensit's lodger? If I had been willing to spend some time getting to know him, even going down to the pub with him, perhaps I would have found that he was very lonely – a fact that looking back now is quite likely. If I had not been so busy looking after myself perhaps I could have helped him to know Jesus. Perhaps our evangelism is limited because we spend so much time with Christians. We never actually get to know at any depth those people who are still searching. I suppose it is only when we get to know them and bother to listen and understand, that we will really be able to share the faith we have. So really it is not only we that lose out when we choose the safe and comfortable things but also that we limit our potential to spread the good news. Perhaps Jesus is actually calling us out of the armchairs of our accepted thoughts and tradition to sit on the pilgrim's folding stool. (I don't know where I got that from!) But how? If we are going to get involved with all sorts of people, how do we protect the truth? It's so easy to get led astray. I suppose that is what the personal walk with God is all about, that's where the Holy Spirit comes in, we need to keep close to God so that although we are open to people, we do not just accept everything they say.

Well, Auntie Flo, I seem to have finished up with as many questions and loose ends as ever. It is very challenging, though, and I am sure that God is teaching me something through it all. Thanks for bearing with me.

Love to you again, and God bless you,

David

14: Differences

Dear Antie Flo,

Do you remember me telling you about my friend Jill Pritchard? She is the one who objected to our Sri Lankan sewing-machine project, and in fact it was she, I suppose, who got me involved in this anti-flow idea. Well, I had a long chat with her the other night after the house group meeting. She invited me to take her home! At least she needed a lift home and suggested I might give her one. We got chatting about things and I told her of my encounters(!) with Ron, and his call for people to get involved. Which, as you can imagine, she heartily agreed with. I said that what troubled me was how to know who to get involved with (and who not to get involved with). We had arrived at her place by this stage so she invited me in for coffee, I went in hoping she hadn't got the wrong idea of what I meant by getting involved with people! While the kettle was boiling, we continued our discussion.

'Doesn't getting involved mean compromise?' I asked. 'I know for instance that the local Council of Churches World Development group (which Jill is involved in) not only has people from other Protestant churches on it, but also Catholics. If you don't believe the same things how can you work together?'

'Well,' said Jill. 'You work on the basis of those things that you can agree on. You concentrate on those aspects and not the disagreements. Now that is not to say that there are no differences and we can't sweep those under the carpet. But the areas of possibility are much greater and as you get to know and understand each other you even find that some of the differences are only based on misunderstandings. It is a question of respecting each other and our differences, without hiding from them or

COMMUNIST ACTIVIST
USELESS UNEMPLOYED
BOOZY CATHOLIC
BLACK HOOLIGAN
JUST A HOUSEWIFE

denying them, and then getting on with what we can do.'

I suppose the other factor, when you think about it, is that we all compromise the truth! None of us is perfect so we cannot know or have the absolute truth. We need to believe that we are moving nearer to the truth all the time, with God's help, but we have not arrived. Insights that other people bring us, both those who are Christian and those who are not, may actually be sent by God to help us – and them – on the way. Therefore, I suppose, that respect for, not blind acceptance of, others' viewpoints is very important.

Jill was saying that the stereotypes by which we label people are suspect. I suppose it is another aspect of the safe and familiar: we put people into boxes. For example, we Protestants seem to reckon that Catholic priests are only interested in booze and bingo. Yet she said that the local Catholic priest was one of the most spiritual men she had ever known. I thought back to my landlady, Miss Greensit, and the little box in which I had put her priest when she mentioned him. It certainly hadn't been marked 'spiritual leader'! And yet he is probably the very guy Jill was talking about.

'OK,' I said, 'so we can't write off everybody who doesn't have the same theological pedigree as us. But at least they do believe in God – well most of them anyway! How can you get involved with those people who might even be anti-Christian? Surely if our aim is to bring people to a living relationship with Jesus then we can't work with people who are trying to stamp out Christianity – communists for example.'

'But hang on,' said Jill, waving her mug of coffee at me and spilling half of it on the carpet, 'getting people to come into a living relationship with Jesus is not the only thing we are trying to do. We are not helping people so that we can lead them to Jesus. Helping people, getting involved with them, is a valid thing in itself – both for their benefit and for what they can teach us. It is not simply a way to get them to listen to us, it is something that Jesus calls us to in its own right. It's true that they are more likely to listen to us when we share our faith with them in that relationship, but to say that is the aim is to devalue people and see them only as "walking souls".'

Another point chalked up to the lady with the expressive hands.

'OK,' I said, 'if I concede that point, where does that leave us?'

'Well,' she said, 'it means that you can work with people who share at least the same general aim as yours on the social front, even if they do not share your motivation as a Christian. God can and does work through non-believers. What's more, it gives you an opportunity to share the faith with them as well!'

'Right,' I said, 'now what about politics? It seems to me that a lot of the things that you and Ron talk about are to do with politics. I take the point that we have to change attitudes and people's understanding but we also have to change the structures and surely that is to do with politics. I don't think you can mix politics and the Christian faith. We can't say that there is one Christian political party. Christians differ on their understanding of various issues, and no one can say which is the more Christian stance. Not only that, but politics is a pretty dirty game with all those people in it really only for their own benefit.'

I thought Jill's arms were going to take off at this point, they flapped around so much. She did in fact get up and do a remarkable impression of a caged bear. 'You really amaze me at times!' she said.

You don't exactly leave me unsurprised, I thought.

'Politics might be a dirty game,' she continued, 'but how do you think you can just opt out of it? Didn't you learn anything from our Sri Lankan tea discussions? Deciding to do nothing doesn't mean you opt out, it means you support the status quo, supporting things as they are now means that you let the tea-picker be paid low wages in your name. In the same way, the government policies that create unemployment, or perpetuate bad housing or whatever are being carried out in your name, whether you think you are opting out or not. Jesus did not run away from difficult situations: he faced up to them. Politics is pretty dirty and can be abused, but I think that proves how important it is. The more there is at stake, the dirtier the tricks get.'

I wasn't sure that I was getting anywhere on that tack, so I said, 'What about going back to where we started? Who can we work with, how can I join a political party when I know that there may be aspects of it that I will not agree with even if over all it's the closest to a Christian view?'

Jill paused on that one. 'Well,' she said, 'it's a question of tactics. It's like joining a particular Christian denomination. You may feel it is the right one over all, but there may also be aspects of it you don't quite agree with. However, you are going to be far better off joining it than you would be if you went along on your own looking for the 'perfect church'. Anyway, who says your idea of the 'perfect church' is right to start with? It's the same with political parties. You are likely to get far more done if you join one of the well-established parties than if you try to do things on your own. But it's true that it's likely to involve compromise. You have to let some things go in order to concentrate on other priorities.'

I told Jill about the encounter that the lads down in Brice had with the police. I really felt annoyed about that and felt that perhaps I ought to get involved in a political party and try to get them to make the police more accountable to the community. She said that I was missing out on a whole area of politics if I thought that was the only way to do something about such issues.

'You can be a politician without being a member of a political party' she said. 'Holding meetings, writing letters, signing petitions, organising demonstrations, talking with the media is all part of politics. Public opinion is what should influence the parties. I suppose being an independent politician in that way frees you from the constraints of the party and helps you respond to the particular needs of the poor. You could even be elected to a council on such an independent ticket. Though political parties need Christians in them to influence the way that they go, even though it might involve compromise.'

By this time it was getting late so I got up to go. At least this time Jill and I parted on relatively friendly terms.

Anyway, there we go, Auntie Flo, that will have to be the end of another of my short notes to you. It is funny to end talking about compromise as if it were a fact of life. I would have shuddered at the thought of that word a few months ago. Don't get me wrong though, Auntie, I'm not contemplating compromising those things that are the very basis of our Christian faith – I suppose it is sorting the wheat from the chaff that is the problem, deciding what is immovable and what isn't.

Well there is something else for you (and me) to think about. I hope that you are keeping well and that the leg isn't playing up too much. I also hope your cold has gone by now. I had one not so long ago which seemed to drag on for ages.

Well, look after yourself and send my love to the crowd at South Street.

Love David

15: The million dollar question

Dear Auntie Flo,

Sorry I haven't written to you for a while, but life has been rather hectic. First the good news – I've been promoted! You might remember me telling you when I first started that I would have to spend some time in the office just getting to know the ropes and working my way up. Well, the boss seems to feel that the ropes and I are best friends now and it's time for me to move out! While in the office I have been dealing with the bread and butter work of insuring cars, houses and so on. Now I can go out and develop contacts I have made through that and begin to sell the big money-makers – such as life insurance. I get a commission on these as well as a basic wage, so there is a fair amount of motivation to get out and get selling. This is the job that I have been waiting for, it's really the reason why I moved here. It will give me more responsibility, I will get out and meet all sorts of people, I'll have a fair degree of independence and there is the potential to make a lot of money. So you'd think I'd be over the moon, wouldn't you? Well, now for the bad news – I'm not, and I don't think I even know why.

I will try and explain. A few evenings ago – in fact the day I found out about my promotion – I was having dinner with Sandy and Diane Prime. Of course I couldn't contain myself and told them all about the promotion, the sort of work I'd be doing, the better money and so on. They were delighted for me and we talked all about it, what I would be doing, potential contacts, training courses and so on. By the end of the evening I felt really good and pleased with myself. I had begun to think about what I could do to improve the flat and had even begun to fantasise about changing the car. (You would think I had

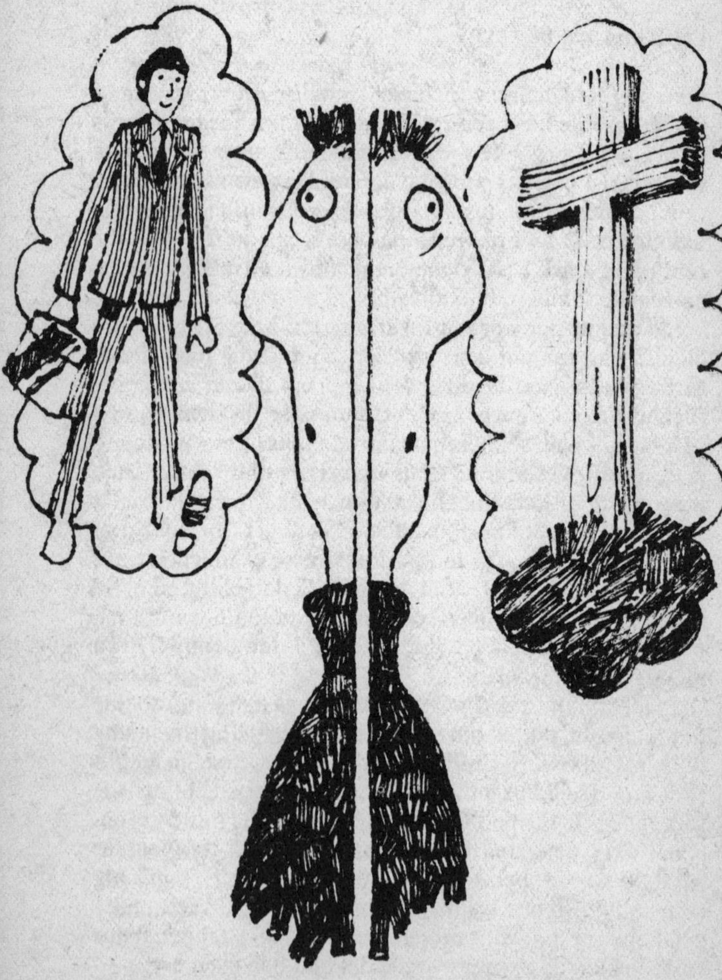

won the pools or something!) What's more, I felt somewhat closer to Sandy and Diane again, a relationship that has, I think, been under a certain strain for the past few months. So, a feeling of *bonhomie* as they say, and well done thou good and faithful insurance salesman, slap on the back . . .

Last night I went round to see John and Amy Wilson to share my good news with them. I told myself that when I got there I should try to contain my enthusiasm for a while, talk about the weather, the kids and that sort of thing, just so as not to seem like an overgrown school kid. I decided that I'd let it nonchalantly slip into the conversation that I had been promoted, then we would have the squeals of glee, hug, hug, break open a fresh bottle of milk, etc. etc.

However, as soon as I got there I felt uneasy. Not because of anything they said or did, but because of me. As I sipped my coffee, I suddenly realised that I was being faced, probably more starkly than ever before, with a basic inconsistency in my life, and it was painful. Being there with John and Amy reminded me of all the discussions that we have had about anti-flow concepts. Being persecuted for the faith, identification with the poor and the oppressed, buying a car that I needed and not what looked good and so on – basically, taking my pointers from being a new person in Jesus Christ and not from the ways of the world. Faced with those real memories I did not feel I could enthuse to John and Amy about my success as an insurance salesman, the increase in wages it was going to bring me, the grandiose plans for the flat or even, to my own horror, the thoughts I had about a new car. I suddenly realised that dinner with Sandy and Diane Prime, people with a lifestyle which, until I came here I would have wished to copy, had allowed me to slip back into my old way of thinking. Looking back to dinner with the Primes, I realised how easy it is to stay safely with those whose outlook we share and to ignore anything we might find uncomfortable in what is going on around. The values of the world and its views of success and progress work so insidiously that we can easily compromise for the sake of our own comfort. It can become easy to rationalise almost any excess.

It looks terrible when I write it down. Seems as though Sandy and Diane are some sort of unfeeling ogres with an astonishingly luxurious lifestyle. Yet they are not like that at all. They are really very ordinary middle-class, Christian people with, as I say, a lifestyle that most of us in that sort of category would aspire to. They are not flashy, but certainly have very set ideas about what standard of house and furnishings they want, and they are willing to work hard, save and get what they want – all very laudable in a way. They think about the poor, but I suppose in that uninvolved way that Ron talks about. Giving a bit of money to some organisation to look after the poor for them. They are very nice people but, as I'm sure you will have picked up even before this episode, they don't really go for this anti-flow idea.

I can see now that I'm really at something of a watershed in my life. I could go for this job in a big way, make plenty of money, give some of it away to various groups and stick close to Sandy and Diane. With them and others at Claygate I could learn to live happily and even justify my position both socially and theologically. But I have been through so many experiences since coming here – and I don't think they will let me rest easy if I opt for that future. The Lord has opened my eyes to a whole new area of discipleship and I can't just shut them again. If I did, could I still say that I was following his will?

As I sat there with John and Amy talking about everything but work, I realised that I was faced with some big decisions. I could not ignore them, nor put them off. If I carried on as I was, got busier at church and through the promotion at work, building up my own little world, then I would actually be making a positive decision to ignore all that has happened in these past months, and to support a safe and socially acceptable Christianity.

I think that John and Amy sensed the change in my mood as soon as I arrived and that something was not quite right. Looking back now I can see that they fished around with leading questions until they hit on it by asking how things were going at work. I poured it all out. As usual they were pretty level-headed in their reaction.

'First of all,' John said, 'we can't just withdraw from the financial system that we have. We might not like the vast differentials of pay that there are and some of the things that industry and commerce get up to. But the commercial world exists and our task is not to withdraw from it completely, but to try and change it. We can't all be social workers or youth workers; after all, someone's got to create the wealth we live by. The real problems lie in the way that wealth is created, how it is distributed and the effects that that has on the poor and powerless. We start to tackle those problems by looking at our individual way of life: the way in which we get our wealth, how we use it, and what we do with our time.'

'That's right,' said Amy, 'if you are only going after this job because of the good money (even if your intention is to give some away) and the status, then you are likely to put so much energy into it that you will have no time to keep your contacts down in Brice for instance. Because you don't have the time to keep in contact with this new way of thinking then you will slip into justifying all sorts of home comforts because you are so busy.' (Like my experience with Sandy and Diane, I thought.)

'If you measure success only by your job,' she continued, 'then you miss out on all the other aims we should have as Christians. Our ideas of success have to incorporate our response to the injustices in the world, including those in our own back yard. If you spend all your life making a success of your job, then you are left with little or no time to follow Jesus in hearing and identifying with the poor and oppressed, no time to hear what their problems are so that you can try to change the unjust system in which you live and work.'

'What's more,' said John, 'you have no time to make friends with people who are not Christians and to share with them the good news of Jesus Christ. You know evangelism is most often hindered because we as Christians are too busy at our work and our churches to actually have time to talk about Jesus. We plan campaigns of evangelism and invite in evangelists but they will be most effective only when we have done the groundwork in the context of costly relationships with people.'

'So,' I said, 'It's not necessarily wrong to do the job but it's the attitude we have to it and the priority it takes in our thinking?'

'That's fine and right,' said John. 'Though I would say that *some* jobs are rather suspect, but you have to work that out for yourself. And most jobs do mean that we have to work thirty-five or forty hours a week at least, which does not leave much time for doing other things. This is doubly problematic when you think of the many people out of work. As Christians together we should be able to sort out some way of sharing jobs and wealth and freeing some people's time for work in the community or church. Acting like a city on a hill, as it says in the Bible, showing people what is possible. If Christians and the church did become more like signs of the kingdom I am sure that too would remove some of the barriers that prevent people getting to know Jesus.'

'I agree with you about that,' I said, 'but how are we supposed to free people to do this sort of work?'

'Well,' said Amy, 'we, for instance, have been thinking over the last few months that perhaps we ought to have some other Christians living with us here. We own this big house which is more or less sorted out now, so we could easily have someone else living here, or even another couple. We could share our resources – even share our money – then with only one mortgage, one washing-machine, one car etc., we would not need so much to live on and therefore we would not need to earn so much. So one of the people could perhaps have a part-time job or no job at all. Then they would be free to work in the community. Perhaps we could use the house as a place that's always open to people with particular problems or whatever. Some people have the sort of job it would be impossible to do part time but this way of living would mean they would keep in contact with what is going on and their earnings would go into a common purse. It takes the purely personal aspect out of earning.'

Well, I can see the point, but really I am not so sure that I want to live in community like that. I value my independence and I said so.

'I know that I can become very self-centred living alone, but is there no way in which I can live in my own flat and yet still show a responsibility for others in the Christian community and with them for the wider community?' John and Amy saw the point and agreed that not everybody would want to live in community so we went on to look at the alternatives.

We came up with the possibility that groups of Christians with concern for a particular problem could work together. They could pool some of their resources and perhaps pay one of their number to work with them full time. Now, rather than just having a standing order at the bank and forgetting about it, they would meet on a regular basis to support this project. Let's say a group has a concern for young people who have been in trouble with the police. It may be that one of the families has or buys a house larger than their needs. They agree to act as a base for the project while another person is supported financially by the group in order to spend his time contacting and working with these young people at risk. He (or she) lives in the base house and uses it as a home to bring or meet the young people. The family in the house would be involved in some of the face-to-face work, while still having some 'private' rooms in the house. Perhaps another person might also be living there but spending half his time with the project and the other half in a job. The rest of the support group would meet with the whole group on a regular – perhaps weekly – basis, their task being to find out what's happening, give financial support, pray for the project, drop in at odd times to talk to people who might be around, and work on specific limited tasks or contacts with specific young people. So all those involved would recognise a personal responsibility to each other, the project and the young people at risk. They would not just be working and earning for themselves, but would be entering into costly committed relationships with others and identifying with those in need. John, Amy and I felt that all these things are important if one is to keep a real anti-flow view on life. As I had already seen, it is too easy otherwise to slip into the way of the world.

Well at about this point in our discussions a persistent wailing came from the kids' bedroom and John disappeared upstairs to sort the children out. While he was out I asked Amy what the idea was behind John's rather pointed remarks that he thought some jobs were 'suspect' and that I would have to work that out for myself! Amy smiled and told me that John has a thing about insurance and an even bigger thing about insurance salesmen! He had never actually said anything to me, though, because he thought it would be rather embarrassing all round! But he feels that if we as Christians did feel responsible towards each other then we would not need insurance. If people were left without something, then they would be supported by the fellowship. Playing on the need to be able to immediately replace all that we ever have is a real pandering to our materialistic tendencies. He also feels that some insurance salesmen are guilty of persuading people to buy policies that they neither want nor need! So that was a bit of a bombshell, but before I could say anything John arrived back in the room, children duly settled. Amy told him what we had been talking about at which he smiled and did indeed look rather embarrassed.

'It's not just insurance salesmen,' he said hastily. 'I think that there are a lot of sharp practices in business and some Christians could be accused of not seeing the link between their faith and their business practice, however unintentionally. Whether we need insurance is another issue really and given our present lack of commitment to each other it is perhaps a wise precaution, in moderation! Though perhaps the sort of scheme we described before would reduce the need for it as we increase our commitment to each other.'

'What about insurance salesmen then?' I asked. I wasn't going to let him get away with that one without more of an explanation. 'We're not all rogues, you know, we have a certain professional pride.'

'I'm sure you do, but you're spurred on by the commission you get, and if your prime motivation in life is to be successful in your job, you are likely to want to break the targets, are you not? We all look for success, after all.'

'Well I suppose that's true,' I said, 'but you make it sound as though we only think of ourselves all of the time.'

'Well isn't that one of the great dangers in life?' said John.

I could see anti-flow creeping up on me again.

'So,' I said. 'The important factor is what yardstick we use to judge success. If it is simply in terms of work and not of our contribution to society as a whole, we not only corrupt our own values but perpetuate a corrupt system as well?'

'That's it,' said John, 'you've got it – and it is also time I went to bed.' So with that subtle hint I bid them goodnight and left with, as they say, a load on my mind.

If I keep my job and my flat with Sandy and Diane Prime how am I going to prevent myself succumbing to the subtle pleasures and comforts of middle-class suburbia? I suppose the million-dollar question is – how am I going to be a new being in Christ, in the world but not of it, in short an anti-flow person?

That, Auntie Flo, is the question.

Love David

Discussion starters

The first part of the following sections contain questions based on each of the letters and could be worked through alone. However it would be more beneficial to do this with a small group of people, say eight or ten of you learning from each other.
The second part of each section contains various ideas for groups. It has long been acknowledged that people gain much more from 'doing' than from just talking and listening. The activities are not just for young people, once over the initial embarrassment, groups of any age will enjoy getting involved.
The questions from the first part can be followed and talked through in the context of the activities. You do not need to do all of the questions or all of the activities. You may find that your group is interested in some aspect of a letter that is not covered, ask them first!
Some of the sections need a little preparation – sending off for information or bringing materials – get your group to do this. Where large sheets of paper are needed, rolls of lining paper from the wallpaper shop are a cheap source.
Get members to read the relevant letter before you meet. Use the bible passages in the letters and notes to inform your discussion. Spend time in prayer, not just a formal beginning and end but a real time of sharing before God.

Most of all – enjoy yourselves!

1 & 2: Settling in and seeking the faithful

1. What sort of a person do you think David is?
   Do you see anything of yourself in him? Do you react in the way David does to things that are different? Are you open to learn and to change?
2. Do you ever ask yourself the question, 'How am I a new being in Christ?' What is the difference between you and other people at your work, not in what you say but how you live?

Group work

Do all your group know each others names and background? If in doubt have four minutes together in pairs, spend two minutes each listening to your partner introduce themselves to you. Then in the full group introduce each other to the other members.
In your pairs construct a collage of cuttings from colour magazines stuck on to large sheets of paper. The collage should depict the life David leads. Explain it to the rest of the group.
Get the group to complete the sentences 'I feel . . .' and 'I think . . .' individually on a piece of paper. Ask them to share their sentences with the group in turn. If they don't want to they simply say 'pass' with no comments from anyone. Ask the group to keep these pieces of paper until the final session when they can look at them again. They could use them as a bookmark. You could keep their collages until the final session as well. They could then look at them and see if there have been any changes.

3: Two sides to a story

1. In what ways are we linked with the people of the Third World?
2. Do you think christians ought to get involved in changing the systems by which we live or confine ourselves to treating and caring for its victims? Should we send sewing-machines or protest about poor wages?
3. What do you think about the W.D.M. tea idea? Which do you think is its most important aspect?
   a. The fairer deal it gives to the workers.
   b. The lobbying for better conditions.
   c. The fact that it constantly brings the issue before our eyes.

Group work

Get members of the group to write for information to the organisations listed below. After your discussions ask them to tell the rest of the group something about the aims and methods of the organisation they contacted. Plan some action, even if it is only further educating yourselves. Perhaps you could individually choose an organisation to get involved with.
You could prepare an exhibition of the material received for the rest of the church, and contact Traidcraft to get a local representative along with Third World goods for sale.

Traidcraft, Kingsway, Gateshead NE11 0NE
World Development Movement, Bedford Chambers, Covent Garden, London WC2E 8HA
Christian Aid, P.O. Box 1, London SW9 8BH

4: Anti-flow

1. What does repentance mean to you?
2. Do you agree with the concept of anti-flow as described in this chapter?
3. With Paul, do you have difficulty in understanding what you do, because you don't do what you want to do, but do what you hate? Romans 7.15. Why does it happen? Can you think of some specific example?
4. Are we sinners only because we have done something wrong?
5. What enables us to change and be anti-flow people?
6. Can you think of examples at home, work or school where anti-flow principles could apply?

Group work

You could get the group to look up repentance in the Bible using a concordance and look afresh at the meaning of it in context. Get each person to write a telegram (or rather a telemessage) explaining what repentance means.
Is your group run on anti-flow principles or do you just follow the normal way of running a group? Are you, for instance, honest with each other about your good and bad points – as the Bible calls us to be?

Try thinking of – and singing – some songs and hymns which deal particularly with repentance.

5: Second instalment

1. Can sin only be present in people? Can a system be sinful?
2. Is it ever right to break the law?
3. Can you think of any specific situations when you believe that by keeping the law we disobey God?
4. How do we ensure that we are doing right and not just breaking laws we want to because of our basic sinful nature?

Group work

Get some of your group to read out the 'conflict stories' from Luke 5.12 - 6.11.

In fours, try and construct a modern day parable based on the story of the Tower of Babel, Genesis 11.

Get each member of the group to copy one bubble of the anti-flow chart onto a large sheet of paper. The writers then hold up their sheets in turn and explain how they see their bubble fitting into the whole picture and whether they agree with it or not.

6: The first test

1. Do you think most people want a better car? If so, why?
2. Do you think there is anything wrong in having a new car, if you can afford it?
3. Do you agree with the suggestion that God wants us to work hard and earn as much money as we can because our prosperity then shows that God is honouring our devotion to him, and it means we can give more money away?
4. Can you take the concept of a responsible lifestyle too far? What are luxuries and what are necessities? Consider David's statement "... We will all be out on the streets living in shanty huts if we're not careful!" Page 43
5. Do we just salve our consciences by saying such things as 'God wants us to have good things'?

Group work

Get the group to 'Brainstorm' the reasons for having a car. That is, get them to call out as many reasons as they can think of – silly and serious, as to what people want from a car. Write them all down as they say them on a large sheet of paper that everyone can see. Then try to isolate which of the reasons demand that you need a new car and could not be met by an old banger. Are the reasons good enough to justify to God the purchase of a new car?

7: Not counting the cost

1. Opponents of Apartheid point to Biblical passages such as Galatians 3 v.28. "So there is no difference between Jews and Gentiles, between slaves and free men, between men and women; you are all one in Union with Christ Jesus." to offer Biblical evidence for their opposition to Apartheid. It has also been stated by a past Archbishop of Canterbury that "The ideal and practice of Apartheid is a denial of God's law of the relation of man to man as, irrespective of colour, created in God's image". Therefore, "All men are equal in the sight of God." Supporters of Apartheid say that the first reference only applied to the spiritual relationship and that in the second case 'equality' is never mentioned in the Bible. Do you think Biblical evidence supports or opposes Apartheid?
2. Have you ever been persecuted for your faith? Looking back, have there ever been times when you realise you should have said or done something but did not for fear of what others may have thought or said?
3. Can you think of situations in this country in which you think Christians ought to take a positive stand, even though it might mean persecution?

Group work

Try a role play with the group. You could base it round a discussion between Mr Asago and his wife as to whether he ought to go and march in a demonstration. Imagine they are still in South Africa, he could be talking about the need to stand up and be counted, she could be pressing the fact that if he is counted once again by the police he may end up dead and who would that help? You could include some of their children and a friend of Mr Asago's or his mother-in-law or whomever, they can decide whose side they will be on and can support the main character. Then try a role play using a situation in England as an example. What are the pressures stopping us being real anti-flow people?

8: The horns of a dilemma

1. Do you believe that violence is ever right?
2. Is a christian concern for justice more important than our principles about violence?
3. Do you agree with the waging of
   a. the Falklands war?
   b. the guerrilla struggle that changed Rhodesia to Zimbabwe?
   c. the resistance movements in Second World War France?

   Do you see any differences between these events?
4. Do you think we will bear any responsibility if the situation in South Africa drives more people to violence?

Group work

The essential elements of the Just War doctrine are listed below. With your group work out whether Mr Asago's arguments fit in with this theory.
Do you agree with the doctrine?
For a war to be justifiable it must:
1. have been undertaken by a lawful authority;
2. have been undertaken for the vindication of an undoubted right that had been certainly infringed;
3. be a last resort, all peaceful means of settlement having failed;
4. offer the possibility of good to be achieved outweighing the evils that war would involve;
5. be waged with a reasonable hope of victory for justice;
6. be waged with a right intention;
7. use methods that are legitimate, i.e. in accordance with man's nature as a rational being, with Christian moral principles and international agreements.

Ask some of the group to find out ways we could help the situation in South Africa and perhaps avoid violence.
For more information contact:
Christian Concern for Southern Africa
1 Cambridge Terrace, London NW1 4JL
Anti Apartheid Movement
89 Charlotte Street, London W1P 2DG

9: Peacemakers

1. What is the big difference between nuclear weapons and so called conventional weapons
2. Can nuclear weapons be justified under the doctrine of a Just War?
3. Do you believe in unilateral or multilateral disarmament?
4. How can we work positively for Peace, to do away with the fear that drives us to arms?

Group work

Ask some members of the group to contact the organisations listed below and to bring along the information they get back.
Ask the group to think of something you could do together which will work towards peace.
Try designing your own peace badge, poster or slogan.
Contact:
C.N.D. and Christian C.N.D., 11 Goodwin Street, London N4
Campaign Against Arms Trade, 5 Caledonian Road, London N1 9DX
Methodist Church Overseas Division, 25 Marylebone Road, London NW1 5JR for PEACE PACK – Cost 40p including postage and has lots of information from the above organisations and others.

10: Work but no job

1. What does it mean to be without a job in our society? Do the answers show up some questionable values we have?
2. What can be the difference between a job and work?
3. Does the present situation of unemployment and general change have to be a crisis or could it be an opportunity?
4. Are unemployed people to blame for being without a job?
5. What can you do about unemployment or its effects?

Group work

Ask an unemployed person in your group or invite an unemployed person in to talk about how it feels to be unemployed. Be sensitive, some people may find it difficult or impossible to do. Work through the above questions with them present as well. If you don't know any unemployed people well enough to invite them along, think about why that is.

Ask people to try and imagine how they would feel if they were suddenly made unemployed. How would they react? Get them to spend some time in silence thinking about it. How would they spend their time? Are there ways your church could work with the unemployed? Contact your denominational headquarters and ask them for any literature they have and information on how you can help.

11: Just a mother

1. Do you think that being a mother and/or a housewife is an undervalued occupation? If so, why do you think that is?
2. Do you think men and women are naturally different (other than biologically), or are they just conditioned that way by society?
3. Do you think that the man should be the head of a relationship? How should that work out in practice?
4. How important do you think the family is in the development of attitudes?

Group work

Have a number of magazines available (Newspaper supplements for example) and in pairs, look through them to see in what roles women are portrayed. Do they reflect the actual situation of women? Do they help keep women in these roles? How do they depict men? Is that accurate? Do the women in your group want to escape their image or are they happy? From a biblical point of view should men and women be happy with the roles in which our society tries to put them?
What different roles do we give to women and men in the Church? Do we reflect a wordly or a biblical view?

12: A white problem

1. Are we all racists at heart? Deep down, do you have 'suspicions' about people of other races – particularly coloured people? Can we justify those feelings from a christian standpoint? Can you think of specific instances where that prejudice has affected your thinking/actions? What can we do to overcome these feelings?
2. How do you rate the work of our police force? Do you think they have a difficult job? Do you believe any of the stories about victimisation of ethnic minorities by the Police? If so what do you think can be done about that, how does it link in with question one? If you don't believe them, why don't you?
3. Is racism in Britain a white person's problem or a black person's problem?

Group work

In groups of three, talk about the positive aspects of Britain's multicultural society. In the full group, make a list of all the good things you have thought of. Do we highlight these aspects enough? What can you do to emphasise the positive aspects. If you do not have many people from racial minority groups in your area, it is probably even more important to do this. What about an 'ethnic evening' with food, music, dance and information from one part of the world. Your missionary society, local Community Relations Council or Christian Aid may help. Using a concordance, get the group to look up some references about Gentiles. Look for the tensions between Jews and Gentiles and how it was pointed out that God's message was for all.
See especially Acts 10. 34-48.

13: The bottom line

1. Jesus said he was chosen 'to bring good news to the poor.' Is the church today associated with the poor and the oppressed? Should it be? See Luke 4. 18-21.
2. If you think it should, how can we get alongside the poor and identify with them?
3. Do you think the church ought only to be concerned with converting people to christianity and that this is what will eventually make the world a better place?
4. Do you think most christians spend too much time with other christians? Do you think this limits our potential for evangelism?

Group work

Get group members to make an individual list of people whom they count as friends. Then ask them to see how many of them are christians. Do they know which of them would call themselves christians and which would not? Ask your group whether they would be willing to organise an exchange with a church group in another part of town which is socially very different from yours. You spend a day with them at their church, attending services, going home for lunch with them etc. Then invite them back to your church.

14: Differences

1. Do you think we all compromise the truth? Is our view absolutely right, our denomination the only true Church?
2. Does God speak to us through non-christians? Can you think of any biblical examples?
3. How can we ensure that we are open to other peoples ideas and yet remain true to the basics of our faith? What are the immoveable basics of our faith?
4. Is helping people of value in its own right or should it only be seen as a step towards bringing people to Christ?
5. Do you think christians ought to be members of political parties? Do you think we ought to lobby M.P.s, go on demonstrations etc? Have you ever done such things? What needs to be at stake for you to get involved?

Group work

In two's, draw your image of a typical minister or clergyman. You don't need to be Van Gogh – matchstick men will do, with labels explaining the parts e.g. big hand to hold collection plate etc! Share these with the rest of the group.

Discuss whether that 'typical', somewhat comical person actually exists in real life, or are the ministers you have known quite human? Think of other people for whom we have stereotyped images who are actually quite different when met 'in the flesh'. People of other denominations, ethnic origins, policemen, tramps etc. Do members have any 'before and after' experiences to relate?

15: The million dollar question

1. How important an affect do the people we mix with have on the way we think?
2. If we disagree with something should we withdraw from it completely or try and change it from within? How do we stop being seduced by its attractions? What role can the church play and particularly small fellowship groups, in helping us in this struggle?
3. Is your prime concern to make money and work for a better lifestyle or to serve God and other people? Do you think these things can conflict? Do they conflict in your life? Do you think that any of the schemes for greater commitment to each other and to the community which are suggested in the letter could work?
5. Look at Acts 4 32-36 and see how the early christians lived. Is that relevant today?

Group work

Ask the group to make collages/drawings in pairs of how they see David's life now. Compare them with the collages made at the first session, what are the differences, how has David changed?

Ask the members to complete the sentences 'I feel . . .' and 'I think . . .' Ask them to read out what they wrote in the first session and what they have written now. How have they changed? Have they changed their views on any issues or on being a disciple of Jesus? Have their feelings about the rest of the group changed? How will this affect their future life patterns?

Suggested further reading

The Call to Conversion, Jim Wallis *Lion 1981*
Radical Discipleship, Chris Sugden *Marshalls 1981*
Rich Christians in an Age of Hunger, Ronald Sider *Hodder 1980*
Bias to the Poor, David Sheppard *Hodder 1982*
Poverty, Revolution and the Church, Michael Paget Wilkes *Paternoster 1982*
God's People in God's World, John Gladwin *I.V.P. 1980*
Bring Forth Justice, Waldron Scott *Marshalls 1982*

Also published by Marshalls

RADICAL DISCIPLESHIP

Chris Sugden

Christ is living amongst us. Not in the churches of the English middle-class but in the slums of Bombay, the horrors of Cambodia, the savage feudal wars of Central America. He is the same today as he was 2 000 years ago, when he made friends with the outcasts, the lepers, the prostitutes, the tax-collectors, and condemned the Pharisees for their hardness of heart.

We crucify him every day we do not protest against the evil which allows two thirds of the world's population to starve, which allows oppression, injustice, racial and class prejudice to rage unchecked, every day in which we do not alleviate their suffering and pray that our indifference might be forgiven.

We can only truly experience the liberating freedom which the cross brought if we surrender to the demands Christ makes of us. Isn't it about time we stepped down from our pedestals, got our hands dirty and took the whole gospel seriously?